WISDOM

The Forgotten Factor of Success

To
Richard
& His one as well!

By the same Author

Secrets of Super Achievers

Wisdom - The Forgotten Factor of Success

All enquiries regarding this publication and Philip Baker's speaking engagements, to be made to:

Webb & Partners

Post Office Box 1339, South Perth, Western Australia, 6951.

Telephone: (08) 9367 2190

Printed by McPherson's Printing Group, Maryborough, Victoria, Australia

National Library of Australia, Canberra, Australia.

ISBN 0 646 34483 8

DEDICATION

To Ron and Pat

You will never really know the difference you have made in our lives.

Thank you.

CONTENTS

Section I . THE ANATOMY OF WISDOM

Section II . THE ASPECTS OF WISDOM

Section III . THE APPLICATION OF WISDOM

THE ANATOMY
OF WISDOM

Chapter 1
THE MANY FACES OF WISDOM

The title of Lawrence of Arabia's celebrated book, The Seven Pillars of Wisdom, indicates an important truth. Namely, that the subject of wisdom contains many aspects, nuances and disciplines. The stuff of which wisdom is made is rich and varied. It cannot be contained with simple definition. Dictionaries attempt to give us an overall impression yet they merely present the lay of the land. Its depth and contours are only revealed as we dig.

The Oxford dictionary defines the word as:

'Being wise, soundness of judgement in matters of life and conduct.'

Whilst Webster puts it this way:

'The quality of being wise. The faculty of making the best use of knowledge, experience and understanding.'

Both these definitions hint at the difference between wisdom and knowledge. The latter is about the accumulation of information whilst the former has more to do with conduct, judgement and living. One focuses more on intake, the other on output. One is concerned primarily with education, the other with application. We live in a world, however, where these distinctions are not made obvious. Passing exams at school or university is all very well, but wisdom will help build effective marriages, businesses, churches and nations.

Many mistakenly muse that with memory banks filled with knowledge they have the ingredients necessary for success. Yet, life is not a game of Trivial Pursuit. Life is more like chess. Knowledge is required, but foresight, cunning and intuition are more essential. The complex world we live in does not become subservient and pliable to simply the weight of impressive facts and figures. Life is not like painting by numbers. The canvas is blank. The choices of colour and style are overwhelming and whether we produce a masterpiece or a mess, art or scribble, is all a matter of whether we can plumb the depths of our own soul and tap into its well of wisdom.

The thinker, philosopher and the coffee shop conversationalist may be smart boasting IQ levels into the stratosphere, but whether they are wise or not remains to be seen. Wisdom is, as wisdom does. The translation of knowledge into the stuff of living is the acid test of authentic wisdom. Wisdom is not something you get from a three-step formula in the latest best seller (I should hasten to add that this volume will point you in the right direction: so please don't put it down!).   It is not gained as easily as a diploma or a degree.   No, wisdom has something to do with the soul.   It comes from within.   Any input such as education, reading or relationships simply fertilise and water the growing plant.   The seed, and thus the potential for wise living, dwells deep within us all and will only be released by decision, discipline and the desire to explore and organise our inner world.

Wisdom is not a skill that is learned.   Neither is it about information that is acquired.   Knowledge is well and good in its own place, but wisdom is an essential for successful living.   The ancient Book of Proverbs calls it 'The Principal Thing' and enjoins the reader to drop all else in its pursuit:

'Search for her as you would hidden treasure.'[1]

The reason for this is manifest.   Wisdom leads to all other things.   You desire a successful business, a vital marriage or continued growth in character, then wisdom is what you need.   If you plan to navigate through life's troubled water, through relational or circumstantial pain, then wisdom is an essential ally. Wise people have always realised this and always will. Therein lies the rub. Wisdom recognises its own indispensability.   Foolishness is blind to such matters.

Proverbs again makes the point well, that the first sign of wisdom is seen in the desire and early pursuit of it.² The fool is by definition one who never starts on the quest. 'Wisdom is for the birds', he retorts, 'Why waste my time and effort on its discovery?' This kind of short-sightedness, this failure to discern what is important in life is the essence of inner ignorance. The thirst for wisdom and its slow attainment are essentially matters that flow from the deepest parts of our being.

Knowledge concerns the head, whereas wisdom proceeds from the heart and only the heart can truly engage on the journey that is wisdom. Those who travel this road find their speed increasing. They realise that the act of travelling, growing and moving forward is what wisdom is all about. The destination is discovered enroute and each horizon sparkles anew, with further allure and depth, encouraging the pilgrim onward.

STUPIDITY IN HIGH PLACES

One of the primary reasons many do not exert themselves in the quest for wisdom is due to a pervading sense of unworthiness. With enough sense to get through the day, any desire for more is seen to be either unnecessary or overly ambitious. The province of wisdom is often seen as the province of lords, princes and gurus. A noble science needful only to noble lives.

Such objections may spring from an underlying laziness or apathy, but more often than not proceed from a poor self-esteem and a lack of understanding as to the availability of this wonderful gift. Thus we muse that kings like Solomon, or sages like Confucius, have rightful claim to it, but we mere mortals do not. The plain fact of the matter is that the powerful are not always wise, they are not even mostly wise. Rarely is this virtue seen in the life of political leaders.

Nietzsche went as far as to turn this observation into a principle:

'In individuals insanity is rare, in groups, parties, nations and epochs it is the rule.'[3]

Barbara Tuchman, in her excellent book, 'The March of Folly', reiterates this truth:

'A phenomenon noticeable throughout history, regardless of place or period, is the pursuit by governments of policies contrary to their own interests. Mankind, it seems, makes a poorer performance of government than of almost any other human activity. In this sphere, wisdom, which may be defined as the exercise of judgement acting on experience, common sense and available information, is less operative and more frustrated that it should be.'[4]

Personally, I don't totally agree with Ms Tuchman. It's not that our leaders are more stupid than everyone else, it's just that their stupidity seems magnified.

Firstly, because we are all watching them and any foolhardy act today is CNN's main story within half an hour. Secondly, we expect that the larger the decision the more wisdom is available.

I may struggle with the decision to lease or buy a vehicle and in the end just take a plunge in one direction or the other; but in the back of my mind there is an awareness that such a decision is not epic and a mistake is of small consequence. Yet if the decision affects millions of lives then surely the convictions are stronger.

Wisdom, if present, should speak with a louder voice. Unfortunately, this does not seem to be the case. I have a friend who has the opportunity to spend a reasonable amount of time with President Clinton and thus has observed first hand the inner workings of the White House. He once told me what alarmed him the most was the precariousness of key decisions. It seems that a chance conversation in the hallway, a magazine article read the night before, can turn the tide and change an attitude or opinion of those who wield the power.

Such arbitrariness in high office is alarming, yet how else did we expect it to be? Even a cursory study of history shows this has been the case throughout time. One thinks of Churchill and Stalin dividing up Europe towards the end of World War II on a paper napkin in a hotel restaurant. In seconds the fate of millions was changed and Churchill probably felt the responsibility and weight of such a decision as much as we would the choice of a school for our children.

So then wisdom is not biased to high office. Its presence may be encountered and experienced by all. The first paragraph of the world's most celebrated book of wisdom, the Book of Proverbs, makes the point strongly. The author declares that it has been written for the attainment of wisdom and, *'for giving prudence to the simple, knowledge and discretion to the young. Let the wise listen and add to their learning.'*[5] The youth, the sage, the ignorant, all can lay equal claim on the acquiring of a wise heart.

WISDOM GOES UNDERGROUND

'He stores up wisdom for the righteous.'[6]

Now I do not mean here that wisdom is hard to understand. No, rarely will you find it camouflaged with abstruse, esoteric and nebulous obfuscation. Unlike the previous sentence, in the words of Euripides:

'Wisdom is shown in clearness not in obscurity'.[7]

There is one school of thought today which seems to think that the harder something is to understand and the more tortuous the vocabulary, or outlandish the ideas, the more wise it must be.

The New Age prophet, or the literary critic who prizes incomprehensibility and logical mysticism are simply producing smokescreens for their own lack of sense. For the most part, it is nothing more than intellectual masturbation and yields little of lasting value or practical help.

When I speak of wisdom being hidden, I mean that wisdom is not found on the surface of life. Like all precious things it has to be dug for and searched out. Diamonds or uranium may be purchased after someone else has done the hard work. Wisdom, however, is not available on the open market. A little bit like trout in New Zealand: the only ones you are going to eat are the ones you have caught yourself. Such a ban on the commercial marketing of a commodity has to be government enforced, yet wisdom operates this way by natural instinct. It keeps away from the casual enquirer and only gives itself to the desperate.

There is something about seeking with intensity that reveals a quality of soul. 'Ask and keep on asking, knock and keep on knocking, seek and keep on seeking,'[8] Christ declared. He even went as far as to disguise truth in riddle and parable, so only those prepared to 'nut it out' would understand who he was.[9] At first glance this seems unfair. Surely the wonder of wisdom should be dispersed freely to all. Yet, to believe this is to fail to understand that the non-searching soul has not the capacity to hold or use such a treasure.

The search and the desperation builds a capacity and a responsibility to handle this virtue well, once it is acquired. It is a little like allowing the young chick to make its own way out of the egg: muscles are developed necessary for life. To intervene or reduce the struggle, destroys the life. Suffering, then, prepares us for destiny. Winter for summer. Tragedy for triumph.

The lotto millionaire rarely finds their good fortune adding to quality of life. Indeed, the opposite is more often true. The inner world has not grown sufficiently to support the massive increase in criticism, responsibility and pressure that such an event entails. Personal implosion becomes a distinct possibility because the struggle was not sufficient. The easy road proves to be a dead-end.

ENDNOTES

1   Proverbs 2:4.

2   Proverbs 4:7.

3   Friedrich Nietzsche, *Beyond Good and Evil*, Penguin,
     London, 1990.

4   Barbara Tuchman, *The March of Folly*, Abacus,
     London,1984, p 2.

5   Proverbs 1:4.

6   Proverbs 2:7.

7   Euripides, *Orestes*, 1.397, edited by David Grene & Richard
     Lattimore, University of Chicago Press, Chicago.

8   Matthew 7:7.

9   Mark 4:11 & 12.

Chapter 2

HOW TO BE FOOLISH

One way to think about wisdom is to think about what it is not. I have always been a fervent believer in the concept of learning about anything by studying its opposite.

I am obviously not the only one who learns better from counter-example than by example. It was the elder Cato in Erasmus' Apophthegmata who said:

> 'The wise have more to learn from the fools, than the fools from the wise.'[1]

Michel de Montaigne refers in one of his essays to a lyre-player in ancient times (maybe the Mark Knoffler of his day) who used to require his students to go and listen to a performer who lived across the street so that they would learn to loathe discords and faulty rhythms.[2]

In this way the laws of poverty should suggest the principles of prosperity. Knowledge of what makes me unwell should give me a clearer indication of what will make me better. And why something doesn't work should hint at how it might work. In some fields this concept can create lots of effort over a long time before the solutions become apparent. One thinks of Edison and his thousands of failed experiments, all of which showed him how incandescent light doesn't work, but all were small steps towards that first flicker of a bulb. I believe, therefore, that our understanding of wisdom will be enhanced if we could gain a working knowledge of its opposite: folly. What, then, makes the stupid, stupid? How is a fool foolish? (Please note, I am using the third person, as it is far easier to critique everyone else's lack of sense and conveniently exclude oneself from their number!) The following, then, are universal commands for the unwise. Apparent similarity between any of these points and the past or present action of the reader is purely coincidental! (I must however admit that as I composed each one, I was uncomfortably aware of a vague familiarity with them all...)

SEVEN PRINCIPLES OF FOOLISH LIVING

1. Don't think

The first maxim for the foolish is very simple. (Pardon the pun.) If one is to be unwise, one must

cease from all productive mental activity. It is important to protect the mind from solid food. In the age
of the video, Internet and satellite TV, this is hardly a
difficult thing to do. Yet all is not as it seems. Beware
of the cunning soap opera which, under the guise of
mindless entertainment, will suddenly try to sneak in
a moral somewhere. This is both crass and unbecom-
ing, and this tactic can easily ruin a good sitcom or
adventure movie. Most producers and directors have
realised this now. Some are still tempted to put
meaning into media, but now they do so with greater
guile. They either make the point so subtle that only
the smart spot it, thus protecting the innocent sim-
pleton who would be outraged if he realised his
favourite half hour had been, in this way, either
morally or mentally meddled with. The other ploy
that is used by the powers that be is to teach their les-
son in such an obvious or dramatic way that every-
body thinks that it must be just a joke. The Melrose
Place episode on the pain of adultery, or the beach
scene in Rocky III, are both brilliant examples of this
ploy.

The trick here is not only not to think, but to
avoid anything that would lead to thought. Thus, golf
is in, church is out; movies are fine, museums are
not; the Gladiators work well, geographical or histor-
ical documentaries don't; avoid the finance pages,
revel in the funny pages. Yet one must maintain a
constant vigil. Consider, for example, the case of the
cunning cartoonist who takes it upon himself to
awake the blissful ignorant into thought. The simple
and comical picture draws you in, but, then, the

question is asked, the statement is made and the unsuspecting brain begins to whirr. The political cartoon is probably the most obvious in this. However, it is normally in the wrong part of the paper, and thus easy to spot and easy to avoid. The real culprits tend to be cartoons like The Far Side or Leunig (if you live in Australia), or Snoopy (if you do not). Give these images a wide berth! Many have been stirred from their pleasant, intellectual slumber in the middle of the night by the haunting voice of Charlie Brown.

Now, there are some times in life where thinking seems to be the most natural thing to do. At these junctures, nature conspires against us, and pushes us towards pondering. Events like marriage, the birth of a child, graduation, or mid-life crisis are all designed to hijack the empty-headed life and force it towards inner contemplation. Happily, however, the unthinking soul has several readily available escape routes. The gift of alcohol for example is primarily designed for the quick getaway. Being 'blotto with the boys' is guaranteed to paralyse the beginnings of serious thought.

With a good stag party under our belt, we can happily and unthinkingly enter marriage. Yet as one gets older, other alternatives are discovered. The heavily financed sports car, frantic sex with as many partners as possible, or simply the increasing fervour over the local sports team. All of these things can be effective in distracting our attention and thus deadening our reflections. The main thing is that they have the ability to keep us from thinking about the main things. If they have done that, they have done their job well.

2. Never be serious

I am not suggesting that wisdom is always serious, but if you truly desire to avoid its influence, then making light of everything is a good way to go about it. Beavis and Butthead got it right in this regard. So did the criminals in Monty Python's Life of Brian, as they whistled along to 'Always look on the bright side of life' whilst hanging from their respective crosses. (I suspect, however, the Monty Python team were making one of those clever, you-have-to-think-about-it, kind of films. Anyway... let's not think about that now!) You see, when people begin to get serious, they sometimes can begin to say or think significant things and then wisdom can be just around the corner. Nothing is more honoured in the world of the fool, than the lifelong relationship where there has never been a serious conversation. When ancient kings wanted to escape their troubled and overworked minds, they would call for the court jester. In today's world, if you are unlucky enough not to be a jester yourself, they can easily be found in any party or against any bar. The jesters that technology provides are even more abundant and available. Characters like Kramer, or Basil Fawlty, can now, courtesy of the video player and the multiple re-runs, be in your house every day rather than their scheduled weekly visit. So, avoid that intense look or the furrows of the concentrating forehead, for life is a party and hilarity is an excellent anaesthetic to dull the pain and the depth of reality.

3. Do as you feel

This particular command had excellent air play during the sixties: 'If it feels good, do it,' was the catchcry of the times. Orgies and LSD gave this philosophy room to manoeuvre. If one is to stay within the confines of foolishness, one must base all decisions on the emotion of the moment. Impulse spending, one night stands, quick divorces, are the order of the day. After all, your feelings are all you've got. How else should we make decisions? How else can we determine what would be best? (I'm sorry, I just committed the cardinal sin of the wisdom-avoider: asking rhetorical questions. Such things can lead very quickly to right answers, which in turn point the individual towards destiny, fulfilment and meaning.)

The wonder of living by feelings is that you never have to endure anything. Persistence, commitment and resistance need never be experienced. Feelings allow us to cop out and run away. Pilate chose the easy way, giving in to the emotions of the crowd and taking, thus, the path of least resistance by condemning an innocent man to death and setting free a convicted murderer. The path of least resistance is always down hill and it feels good, the wind rushing through your hair as you head for... well, who cares, I don't feel like thinking about that! No, the important thing is to experience. Didn't Satre teach us that existence precedes essence? That who I am is what I feel.

That the subjective is the gauge for right and wrong, good and evil. My truth is the Truth. So, when I feel like I don't love you, then I must leave you, for feelings are my guide and my governor. Without obeying them I would quickly stray from the road of the idiot.

4. Make stupid friends

'Iron sharpens iron.'

This proverb is often quoted when speaking of the importance of companionship. We become like those around us and synergy is a powerful force towards growth. Two wise people together are invariably wiser, two funny people funnier. (Morecombe and Wise, Laurel and Hardy, Abbot and Costello)

Therefore, two silly people are sillier. I might add that if you are only slightly foolish, the best way to become fully qualified is to become best friends with experts. Their prowess will quickly rub off on you and together you will be able to explore the fair fields of folly. If you begin to tire of their company, do not be alarmed as there are a wide variety of fools available on today's market. In this way you can work your way through an amazing array of nincompoops. There is the sports fool and the religious fool, the health food nut and the weekend party animal. The list is endless as their population is increasing. Many are joining and few escape. Now and again large defections occur, due to war, religious revival or major tragedy. Yet these events are few and far between. Constant supply seems guaranteed, quantity is not a problem and quality doesn't matter.

5. Stick to your guns

Although the Book of Proverbs classifies 'stubborn' as a division within foolishness, this attribute is a must for those who wish to escape from the clutches of wisdom over the long term. The will must be exercised in such a way that no matter how obvious the folly or how crazy the path, nothing will detract or divert us from the course. Such wooden-headedness is highly valued within the company of the simpletons. 'You showed them... they couldn't convince you!' is the cry as you are patted firmly on the back whilst being pulled lovingly deeper into the ditch.

Barbara Tuchman defines such stubbornness in this way: 'It consists in assessing a situation in terms of preconceived fixed notions while ignoring or rejecting any contrary signs. It is action according to wish, while not allowing oneself to be deflected by the facts.'[3]

What a marvellous state to be in. How secure, how confident, the ability to believe in one's own opinions regardless of their veracity.

Let the reader, however, be warned. Such strength of will needs a firm foundation on which to rest. For even the most hardened fool can begin to waver under the intense heat of truth and empirical evidence. There must therefore also be a heavy dose of that much-prized virtue among the dimwits: pride. Only the arrogant will survive, so put your chin up and, in the words of Des O'Connor, 'Walk tall.' Refuse to allow the idea that, maybe you could be wrong, to enter your consciousness. Such pride and stubbornness is best exemplified in King Philip III of Spain, who is said to have died of a fever contracted because he sat too long next to a hot brazier, an iron basket filled with burning charcoal. He was, of course, aware of the problem but was helpless as he overheated himself, for the servant whose job it was to move the brazier, when summoned, could not be found. Thus, to this day, the name Philip III is uttered with hushed tones of reverence at the parties and around the barbecues of the barbarians.

6. Develop a biased memory

The advancement of folly, necessarily requires one to keep a short memory. History is replete with examples of those who were able to stay in their delusions by conveniently forgetting what had happened before. Here, the fool would agree with Henry Ford (who was certainly not one of their number)when he said: 'History is bunk.'

Learning nothing from experience takes a special skill. It supposes that empirical fact is arbitrary and without pattern. It holds to those things which support its view and erases that which does not. Only the moment is important. The future and the past are vanishing mist.

When we begin to actually consider former events and work their lessons into our lives, then sagacity is almost upon us. Samuel Coleridge lamented:

'If men could learn from history, what lessons it might teach us. But passion and party blind our eyes, and the light which experience gives us is a lantern on the stern which shines only on the waves behind us.'[4]

Kennedy learnt from both the overreactions and the many blunders that led to World War I and, so, acted with discretion during the Cuban Missile Crisis. On the other hand, the German experience of the Great War taught little to those at the forefront of its second edition. So, error and foolishness persist due to this well-rehearsed and highly developed form of selective amnesia. The fool must never admit error, so memory loss or revisionism is the order of the day.

George Orwell, in his dark novel, '1984', turned this maxim of folly into government policy. He called it 'crime stop'. 'Crime stop means the faculty of stopping short, as though by instinct, at the threshold of any dangerous thought. It includes the power of not grasping analogies, of failing to perceive logical errors, of misunderstanding the simplest arguments... and of being bored or repelled by any train of thought which is capable of leading in an heretical direction. Crime stop, in short, means protected stupidity.'[5]

7. Criticise continuously

Finally, in order to stay proficient in the art of unwisdom the guns of sarcasm, cynicism and cultivated ignorance must be turned outwards. The ability to criticise that which one knows nothing about must rank as one of the Kingdom of Folly's greatest exports. (I refer, of course, to 'great' as a quantitative, rather than qualitative term.) Criticism enables the simple to feel part of the action, whilst merely spectating. The mouth works overtime and a false sense of importance and significance sustain the spirit. One writer describes such activities like those of a 'eunuch in the harem. He sees what's being done, and he can criticise the technique, but he can't do it himself.' This particular command would probably use more mental energy than any of the others.

This seems paradoxical, but it makes an important point. Contrary to general perception, one must be relatively smart in order to be a fool. It is not the ability of the brain that is the source of stupidity, but the use to which it is put. Prejudices are rearranged rather than analysed. Great performances are put down rather than learnt from. Creativity is used on how not to do things, on escaping responsibility and shirking the tough assignments. Even the memory is fully utilised, its digital banks filled with multiple fields of trivia.

So there you have it. The cultivation of stupidity is not as simple as one would think. Yet do not give up, be encouraged, take heart from the many living examples of those who have gone before us. Hold this knowledge firmly knowing that the continual practice of these seven commands will help foolishness flourish in our lives and prohibit wisdom from ever lightening our door.

ENDNOTES

1   Erasmus, Apophthegmata V, Cato Senior, p 39. As quoted
     by Michel de Montaigne, 'Essay on Conversation', *Four
     Essays*, Penguin, 1995, p 33.

2   Michel de Montaigne, *Four Essays*, Penguin, 1995, p 33, 34.

3   Barbara Tuchman, *March of Folly*, Abacus, London,1984,
     p 6.

4   *Oxford Dictionary of Quotations*, Oxford University Press,
     Oxford, 1992, p 212, No. 14, Table Talk (1835) 18
     December 1831.

5   George Orwell, 1984, as quoted by Geoffrey Race in 'The
     Unlearned Lessons of Vietnam', *Yale Review*, Winter 1977,
     p166, and referred to in Barbara Tuchman, *The March of
     Folly*, Abacus, London, 1984, p 481.

Chapter 3

WISDOM AND TRUTH

Books on wisdom have rarely become immediately popular. Give them a few thousand years and they prove their worth. We are drawn more often than not to the latest murder mystery or trendy cartoon compilation. Volumes on wisdom have a musty smell to them. They remind us of school, teachers, and obscure and irrelevant information. If we read a few snippets, we gain some truth, but it's our day off, we don't want truth, we don't want to think, we want to enjoy ourselves, relax, and turn off our brain. Thus, wisdom lore fights its uphill battle. In an age of speed, it has to be digested slowly. When we want the fast lane, wisdom offers us the bicycle. When we insist on the jet boat it prefers a canoe. But, although the journey takes longer, it will prove both more pleasurable and more profitable.

Many would argue today that the term 'wisdom' is almost meaningless. After all, we live in a world where truth is relative and the desires of the individual are society's prevailing force. The suggestion that certain ways of life, courses of action, values or beliefs are inherently more correct and therefore better than others, is seen as offensive and bigoted. 'My truth is as good as anyone else's truth' comes the cry. Those who would suggest otherwise are deemed arrogant and audacious. Yet whilst all people are created equal, to suggest that all ideas are, is nothing more than philosophical dribble.

I believe there is truth and error, right and wrong, good ideas and bad ideas, and ideas somewhere in between. Wisdom is insistent on this point. It does more than simply suggest that there are better or worse ways to live. It makes its statements with clear-headed imperative. Truth is not something we can mould to our preferences. We can pretend it's not there, we can fight and rally against it, but change it, we will not. The tide of wisdom continues on, while we, Canute-like, find our thrones getting bogged in the sands of denial.

The more you fight, the more it proves its point. You may be reading this and disagreeing. You could even be saying to yourself, 'Such talk is too restrictive, too narrow.' If so, then you are inwardly declaring it not to be true, and have therefore set up your own continuum of right and wrong, correct and incorrect. Certainly it is different from mine in the details; in what we perceive truth to be. Yet we are agreed on the concept of truth itself. It is all a little like saying, 'There are no absolutes!' To which the response should be, 'Are you absolutely sure?'

If a person is diminishing their life with addiction to drugs or alcohol, or devastating their relational world by an out-of-control promiscuity, then one can argue that it doesn't matter, or dying young is more fun, or even that short-term pleasure should be the prevailing consideration. Yet the fact that a life is being destroyed cannot be denied. One can try to avoid or run from truth, but finally its consequences and conclusions are irresistible. It is a lot like gravity. You don't break it, it breaks you. Flight doesn't defeat it, it simply supersedes it for a while but gravity continues on, never changing, never weakening, always present.

C.S.Lewis (the famed author of the Narnian Chronicles) points this out well and shows that all of us deep down accept it even though we say we don't.

'Everyone has heard people quarrelling. Sometimes it sounds funny and sometimes it sounds merely unpleasant; but however it sounds, I believe we can learn something important by listening to the kind of things they say. They say things like this: "How'd you like it if anyone did the same to you?" - "That's my seat, I was there first." - "Leave him alone, he isn't doing you any harm."- "Why should you serve him first?" - "Give me a bit of your orange, I gave you a bit of mine." - "Come on, you promised." People say things like that every day. Educated people as well as uneducated, and children as well as grown-ups.

Now, what interests me about all these remarks is the man who makes them is not merely saying that the other man's behaviour does not happen to please him. He is appealing to some kind of standard of behaviour which he expects the other man to know about. And the other man very seldom replies, "To hell with your standard." Nearly always he tries to make out that what he has been doing does not really go against the standard, or that, if it does, there is some special excuse. He pretends there is some special reason. In this particular case, why the person who took the seat first should not keep it, or that things were quite different when he was given the bit of orange, or that something has turned up that lets him off keeping his promise. It looks, in fact, very much that both parties had in mind some kind of law or rule of fair-play, or decent behaviour, or morality, or whatever you'd like to call it, about which they've really agreed. And they have. If they had not, they might, of course, fight like animals, but they could not quarrel in the human sense of the word. Quarrelling means trying to show that the other man is in the wrong. And there would be no sense in trying to do that unless you and he had some sort of agreement as to what right and wrong are; just as there would be no sense in saying that a football player has committed a foul unless there was some agreement about the rules of football.'[1]

Wisdom, then, is learning how to live better. It's about making judgements and choices that will enhance our existence and the existence of those around us. Wisdom is intensely practical and will urge us to make a choice between physical fitness on the one hand, or laziness and overindulgence on the other. It will have something to say on whether we save or spend, rent or buy, attend church or not, and a whole host of smaller yet significant points. If we listen and act upon its insistence, our lives will be greatly affected for the better.

That muttering you can hear in the background is my wife. For to write is easy, but to do is what matters...

Some ten years ago, we had the opportunity to buy our first house. She felt this would be the best course of action. I... well, I don't know what I was thinking. It might have been a fear of long term commitment to a bank or a notion that to buy would cause a loss of freedom that only us 'renters' enjoy. Whatever the case, I resisted stoutly and we remained as we were. Today, with the benefit of hindsight, I cannot believe I was so stubborn and stupid. (There, Honey, I said it!) Over the following seven years, we moved about nine times as successive homes were sold on us forcing us into an almost nomadic lifestyle. Finally we purchased our own home and to rub salt into the wound, the house we bought was the same type and standard of house we had looked at before, only now it was more than twice the price. So, now I am wise. Yet belatedly so. My wife has begun to forgive me, but I know that in several different ways our life would have been better had we taken the plunge into home ownership when we first were able to.

We must not linger too long on such 'if onlys', for to do so will only result in regret and depression. What we must do is learn from our mistakes, change our attitudes and false belief systems and move on. The lessons we take from such experiences will help us on the road ahead. Yet the 'greatest moment of truth' will be when we realise that the quicker we gather wisdom, the better off we will be. Such wisdom is not so much a skill that is learned, or a new bit of knowledge that is added to our arsenal, but an increase in both our character and capacity. Wisdom's truth is assimilated into who we are, not just what we know. We change as wisdom grows and then, and only then, do we discover the truth that becoming trumps achieving every time. We are human beings not human doings and life is about who we are and reaching for our potential rather than simply knowing more or doing more.

As Antoine de Saint-Exupery, the French author, put it: 'How can there be any question of acquiring or possessing when the only thing needful for a man is to become - to be at last and to die in the fullness of his being.'

To die so, is to die happy, for wisdom is truth and truth is liberating. Let me be quick to point out, however, that whether something makes me happy or not in the short term, is not the measurement of what is right or what is true. Doing the right thing can be vexing and painful at times, but in the long term one sleeps better at night and enjoys the days more.

Katherine Mansfield, New Zealand's most famous author, put it this way:

'I want, by myself, to understand others. I want to be all that I am capable of becoming... This all sounds very strenuous and serious, but now that I have wrestled with it, it is now no longer so. I feel happy - deep down.
All is well.'[2]

So the wise heart continues to fashion the life. The inner world empowers the outer. The private life the public. Life is, in this way, inside-out rather than outside-in. At least, this is what should be the case. Sadly for many, personal power and inner direction have been lost along the way. Peer, media and cultural pressure can easily force us into unnatural forms. We become creatures of our circumstance and captives of our context. We forget that life is not about what happens to us but about how we interpret our surroundings.

This explains the laughter of children on the streets of Calcutta and the suicide rates of our youth in so-called advanced societies. The Book of Proverbs declares: 'Better is a dinner of vegetables where there is love than a fattened ox and hatred.'[3] In other words, that which we deem important in the moment is probably not. Position, prestige, and net worth are not what produces the real stuff of life. No, what really matters is discovered within. The hype and superficiality of our advertising age can cause us to suffer from this loss of perspective. Life is about character rather than circumstance, integrity rather than investments, and spirituality rather than sports cars. The corollary of all this is that if we will give attention and input to that which is inside, to the soul, the ramifications on our day-to-day, 9-5 life, will be immense. What is within, will eventually come out. Therefore, to change a life we must change our own selves. Thus the acquiring, resourcing and nurturing of wisdom should become our primary concern, for as it grows our whole life will flourish.

42

With this attitude the wise grow wiser and without it the fool becomes more foolish.

ENDNOTES

1   C.S. Lewis, *Mere Christianity*, Collins, Glasgow,1952, p 15.
2.   *The Letters & Journals of Katherine Mansfield*, Penguin, London, 1977.
3   Proverbs 15:17.

THE ASPECTS
OF WISDOM

Chapter 4

ACTION

The Wisdom of Doing

Wisdom is best defined not in theories, ideas or learning, but in the application of knowledge. Wisdom is action. The learned know but the wise do The power of one idea acted on today can affect millions tomorrow. There are many scholars and scientists whose theories are made impressive by book credits and degrees, but only a few are wise.

Dr Mohammed Yunus of the Grameen Bank in Bangladesh is one such individual. One day in 1976 this Economics Professor strolled through a small village in Bangladesh. He began speaking to a poor woman who was trying to make a living by selling bamboo stools. Although hard at work, she was only making two cents a day. Yunus discovered that the reason for her low profit margin was that she had no capital to buy her own bamboo, so the money was loaned to her by the trader who purchased the final product. The interest charged by the trader essentially removed her profit margin.

On further enquiry the same scenario was repeated in many families within the same village. When Yunus looked at the figures he was both shocked and motivated. Forty-two people were caught in this interest-driven bonded labour. Their freedom would come only if they could borrow the money from more traditional sources. The total amount in question to empower these forty-two people was 856 Takas, about $26.00.

Years later in testifying before the US Congress Select Committee on Hunger, Yunus recalled his intense emotions during this watershed experience: 'I felt extremely ashamed of myself, being part of a society which could not provide $26.00 to forty-two able, skilled human beings who were trying to make a living.'[1]

From this genesis the Grameen (which means village) Bank was founded. Its purpose was to loan money to poor people who had no collateral. The results have been staggering. Over the past two decades, the bank has extended loans in excess of 1.5 billion dollars to some of the poorest people in the world. The bank today serves some two million clients, 94% of them women, with a repayment rate of 97%. Wisdom, when put to work, works.

The wise man in Jesus' parable of the house built on the rock was wise simply because he heard truth and then did something about it. The foolish man is the one who 'hears the words of mine and does not put them into practise.'[2]

Notice that a person is not just wise because they do but because they hear and do. Wisdom requires input, but it is input with intention. Learning with purpose. Studying for its own sake, like any hobby, may be relaxing and fulfiling but does not equal wisdom. It is simply stage one in a two-stage process.

In business, it is not those who have ideas who create profit or change, but those who act on their ideas. We have all had the experience of seeing one of 'our' ideas, which came to us in a quiet moment but remained simply a muse, acted on by another.

I remember my father being mildly upset when a restaurant started putting photographs in their menus. 'My idea. I could have made money if I had gone into this line of business.' My ideas have been similarly hijacked. I mean who of us didn't think of Pet Rocks, Hula Hoops, Trivial Pursuit or the concept of franchising?! Others have had these same thoughts but then decided to do something about them. Doing makes the difference.

Matsushita, probably the greatest entrepreneur of this century, started off by taking this risk of doing. He quit his secure job when just a young man, because his boss disagreed with his idea of creating a new type of light socket. He began to manufacture the product himself. The rest is writ large in the annals of business history. His company now employs 265,000 workers with revenues of 63 billion dollars. Wisdom is seen, not in Harvard or Stanford degrees, but in pragmatic application of well-researched and heart-felt conviction.

Knowledge alone is impotent to change a life. We learn and know, but if we do not act and make a habit of such inaction, we are doomed to discontentment and frustration. We know, but others succeed.

The mere gatherer of ideas will never see the power of wisdom unless they begin to sow in action. Freud smoked so many cigars that he finally had to have the roof of his mouth cut out, and still he could not stop. His biographer, Peter Gay, points out: 'Freud's inability to give up smoking vividly underscores the truth in his observation of an all-too-human disposition he called knowing and not knowing. A state of rational apprehension that does not result in appropriate behaviour.'[3]

F.W. Woolworth is another example of the power of creativity coupled with wise action. He was working as a clerk in a hardware store when his boss began to complain about the piles of out-of-date goods that were not selling. Woolworth's idea was to set up a separate table and price everything at ten cents. Very soon the table became the most profitable area of the store. Woolworth then had the confidence and the wisdom to apply his new idea to an entire store. His boss, however, did not. The Woolworth chain of five-and-dimes quickly spread across America earning him, in the process, a fortune. His former boss once commented, 'Every word I used in turning that man's offer down has cost me about a million dollars I might have earned.'[4]

This characteristic of wisdom has been amply delineated by many writers and speakers. Aristotle to Shakespeare, the Bible to Norman Vincent Peale. Yet we still find it difficult to comprehend. 'Surely there must be more to success than simply doing', we muse. History teaches us, however, that one can lack a high IQ, magnetic personality, or magnificent skill, but if we do something rather than just think about it, a mark is made for all to see.

Often the one most amazed is the doer themselves. William Barclay, a well-known theological writer, is clear evidence of this truth. He was originally approached by Saint Andrews Press, who were wanting to produce a series of Bible commentaries written for the layperson. They asked him whether he would carry out the assignment until they 'found someone good'. (Barclay was a relatively unknown cleric at the time.) It seemed they never could find anyone who was good, and Barclay continued writing until he had finished the entire New Testament. He often made the point that the reason he had been successful was not because he was a wonderful writer or thinker. He admitted there were thousands of others in England alone who had more to say and were better at saying it. The only difference between him and them was that he sat and wrote and they did not. His wife was a useful ally on this point, as she wouldn't let him out of his study for lunch until he had finished many lines.

The same can be said for American Bob Richards, the 1956 Olympic Gold Medal winner in the pole vault. I once heard him say, in an after-dinner speech, that he thought there were a million other men in America who could have beaten him in his event. If raw talent alone was enough he would never have made it to the state championship let alone the Olympics. The story of his life, and many like him, illustrates that success is about what we do with what we have. It is action, not just gifting, the practice and not merely the theory. It is in the arena of action where the wise of heart discover the fruits of wisdom. I am not saying that doing is the *only* thing, as the preceding and following chapters make clear. Yet the point of action cannot be overstressed.

There seems to be something about the concept of wisdom that automatically causes us to picture it only in the study or the library. Wisdom personified is usually the professor from 'Back to the Future' or 'Brains' from Thunderbirds, the bald head of large proportions, the long straggly beard, and the smudges of four-day-old coffee on the jacket. We think these are all dead give-aways to wisdom dwelling within. In reality, however, wisdom comes in varied garb. It is the fourteen-year-old who is motivated by the plight of extinction-threatened tigers, who rallies support from parents, friends, companies and the media, and successfully begins a foundation that actively and practically begins to address the situation. It is the twenty-two-year old young lady from New Zealand who takes the plunge and, with everything she has, launches a computer company just after the stock market crash of 1987. Today her net worth is in the multiple millions simply because of her actions. It is the young American accountant who, because he was unhappy with the council service, won the contract to pick up the garbage in his small suburb. Step by step the small firm grew and was sold several decades later for three hundred and fifty million dollars. All of these real-life examples have come across my path in the last few days. Given time, and a few thousand pages, we could continue in such a vein!

The evidence seems extensive. The best idea in the world not acted upon is merely the idle chatter of the mind. It fills the time but produces nothing. Like trees that fall in the forest when no one is present, so the brainwave without application crashes silently on the shore.

This is not to suggest that wisdom's actions are always productive. Ideas fail, and promising pathways lead to dead ends. The wise, however, are not put off by the small inconvenience of failure. They merely continues to do. Sooner or later the rewards will come. Like the seed in the parable of the sower, some actions die immediately, others start with promise but then shrink and cease when placed under the pressure of the real world, whilst still others have their life drained away slowly as competing forces work against them. But some begin to grow and bear fruit, maybe a little, maybe a lot. If we assume that the four types of soil in the parable all received an equal amount of seed, then we note that only twenty-five percent of that which was sown produced the fruit, and of that twenty-five percent, one-third produced the most fruit. 'Some thirty-fold, some sixty-fold, some one hundred-fold.'[5] When one does the maths, this equates to fifty-three percent of the harvest coming from just eight percent of the seed. From the sower's point of view, though, he is never sure which eight percent will do the job. The rewards may be mediocre, moderate or magnificent. Yet we must continue to sow the seeds of action in our life, for then a harvest of peace and prosperity will be almost inevitable.

The wise, however, unlike the farmer, cannot be judged simply on the harvest. It is the act of doing, not the results of doing, where wisdom is best revealed. Edison's wisdom is seen in the thousands of failed experiments, not just the one that worked. Abraham Lincoln's wisdom was heralded by his growing and impressive list of failures. As he himself once said, 'Success is the ability to go from one failure to the next without losing enthusiasm!' The wise are the ones who are on the road. Destinations reached simply speak of miles travelled.

The road winds on and on. The wise of heart do not falter or return, for the road is right and the journey is fun. The meaning and the thrill are in the process. Some, sadly, never live to see the destination that their words and work finally reached. If they had, it would have proved only a small reward, for wisdom itself provides its own nourishment.

ENDNOTES

1   David Bornstein, *The Price of a Dream*, University Press Ltd., Dhaka, 1996, p 39.

2   Matthew 7:26.

3   Peter Gay, *Freud: A Life For Our Time*, Norton, New York.

4   *Napoleon Hill's Keys to Success*, Editor - Matthew Sartwell, Paitkus, London, 1994, p 168.

5   Mark 4:20.

Chapter 5

RESPONSIBILITY

The Wisdom of Accountability

'Sometimes I lie awake at night and ask, "Where have I gone wrong?" Then a voice says to me, "This is going to take more than one night!"'
Charlie Brown

The opening scene of Forrest Gump was lauded for its special effects wizardry. A computer-generated feather was superimposed on the scene in such a way that the audience believed the camera had caught its long, haphazard and spasmodic movement as it journeyed on the wind to finally come to rest on Forest's shoe.

The feather, of course, was a metaphor. The winds of coincidence and the gusts of chance play a key role on who we are and what we do or don't do in life. However, unlike the feather we can choose how we react to the 'slings and arrows of outrageous fortune'.[1] We can use them to our advantage. In other words, we either use or are used.

The out-of-control life is the life that is responding rather than initiating. It is a life that simply happens rather than is caused. A life which gives in to the lie of fatalism and settles unquietly into the blame mentality.

The truth about Forrest Gump was that he was in control. Other characters in the film with so much more to live for, were often not.

'Que sera, sera,...' apologies to Doris Day, is no way to live. Whatever will be, will be, is to deny humanity the dignity of decision-making and intentional living. Surely destiny and vision have the power to transform lives. Surely choice changes circumstance. Yet we live in a society where many believe that their future is non-flexible, or if it is they are not the ones with the power to flex.

There is a truth that tells us to accept the facts and realise that there are some things we cannot change. This is wisdom indeed, and would keep us from the ditch of despair on the one hand and the dreamland of denial on the other. However, such wisdom may come with a sting in its tail. For who is to say what we can or cannot change? The black and whites are easy here, but most of life is in the grey. Accepting the death of a loved one or the process of aging (even though we fight to mitigate its effects) tend not to be confusing areas for the majority. Yet most of life is not as clear. Sadly however, many place the majority of difficult and painful circumstances into this immutable category; thus avoiding responsibility and losing control.

Reinhold Niebuhr, a key Christian theologian in the 1940s and 1950s, once wrote on the back of an envelope a short prayer that sums up the dilemma we find ourselves in. It became the prayer of Alcoholics Anonymous and is familiar to us all:

'God, grant me the serenity to accept the things I cannot change, the courage to change the things I can, and the wisdom to know the difference.'[2]

Granted, this type of discernment takes work and rigorous self-evaluation. It is a lot easier to sing with Mother Mary: 'Let it be, let it be.' Life, however, is to be lived. We are not meant to be just hitchhiking through our allotted span in these mortal vehicles. This is the passivist approach where life, rather than be caused, just happens. Floating downstream is enjoyable in the short term, but becomes soul destroying in the long term. Significance and fulfilment are not found amongst those who spectate but those who intentionally involve themselves in the process of existence.

This book is all about such purposeful living. Confronting these issues will quickly cause us to realise that the best view is from behind the driver's wheel and not from the back seat. My hope is that the reader will not only think about existence in new ways but be empowered to practically act so that life is enriched and meaning and destiny are unearthed.

The desire to be in control of our own lives is healthy and sound. The desire to be in control of everyone else's life is not. Megalomaniacs and bossy demi-gods aside, the word 'control', when used in this personal sense is wholesome. Yet, this desire is relatively difficult to translate into reality. For many, the concept and dream of self-authority is a forlorn one. The pressures of conformity and the influence of poor self-esteem seem irresistible.

Some are even worse off. They suffer the illusion of self-control. They think they are in charge, but other forces are at work. Like the business person who works his or her way up the corporate ladder unable to see the strings of materialism or prestige which jerk them ever upwards. Only later in life when the ladder top is reached, the discovery is made that it was leaning against the wrong wall.

These strings that bind us are often translucent and hard to spot. Yet we know they are there, for we do not do, that which we desire.

WHO DO WE BLAME?

There seems to me a strange reluctance in our society today to own up to anything. Strange, in that ownership of the problem is also stage one in ownership of the answer. 'It's my fault. I take responsibility,' is not a statement that diminishes, it's a statement that empowers. On the other hand, the pointed finger, as Joseph Brodsky states, is the victim's logo.

The inability to 'fess up' is all too often a sign of personal complacency and an unwillingness to grow, yet grow we must if reaching our potential is our goal.

The tragedy is that many do not realise how far they can go. They have settled for mediocrity and renamed it excellence. They compare only with those who are behind, never with those who are in front. Their hearts are like Japanese Bonsai trees. From close up they seem developed and fully grown, yet to those who look from a wider, more objective perspective, they see what really is, miniatures of what could and should be.

Such an attitude can only be maintained if we find someone or something else to take the rap. The following are the most frequent recipients of our misplaced accusations.

1. God

Homer, in the Odyssey, has Zeus complaining of how humanity point their fingers at the gods as the source of their troubles and suffering: 'It is through the blindness of the humans' hearts' or, as another translation puts it, 'Their greed and folly, that these things come upon them.'[3] Today is no different. Many choose the divine as an excuse for every type of failing or foolishness. Religion becomes the scape-goat upon which we send our volition and intelligence into the desert. Fatalism, and predestination, are allies in this process. These doctrines are, however, all too convenient. The wise heart recognises the truth that, if God is, then responsibility is both His gift and expectation. Free will is protected. We can choose to deny it and say it has been taken from us by the course of nature or by a capricious deity, but

we are the ones who have to choose this escape...
Responsibility cannot so easily be given away.

2. Our Genes

Flip Wilson used to say, 'The Devil made me do it.'
If this is true, then Satan has changed his name to
'gene', for genetics are more and more becoming the
culprit for every form of human behaviour and mis-
behaviour. DNA has got a lot to answer for as it
attempts to swing the nature versus nurture debate,
putting its considerable weight behind the former.

Most prudent researchers and commentators on
this issue would admit to both influences being powerful ones. Our genetics may mix the cement, but the
resultant concrete remains wet for much of life. Our
genes, it seems, can suggest things very strongly, but
they lack the power to make the final act. I might put
on weight easier than you, but genetics don't make
me fat, they only make my struggle with the second
chocolate mousse more painful than yours, you skin-
ny glutton! In the same way, the addictive personality
cannot gain total escape from the prying cameras of
responsibility by hiding behind the screen of 'cellular
make-up'. I may be weak, but I can still say 'no'. I may
be ensnared, but help is normally as close as my
choice. I may discover that my chemical make-up is
such that one glass of wine is never enough, but I
still can refuse that one glass.

In other words, genetic difference should cause us
all to view one another with greater compassion.
Wisdom does not crow over another's failing in an

area of our strength, for we too have our foibles and need the understanding and help of others.

I hate to think what will happen if we begin to apply this new zeal for the chemical code to morality. Such a journey will prove to be on a slippery slope. The adulterer and murderer will breathe easier, but most of society will not. This approach would, however, explain a whole lot of problems. We might discover that our two-year-old is genetically disobedient, while the eighteen-year-old is genetically arrogant. I could point to my DNA as to why I forgot to take out the rubbish, or didn't hear my spouse during that important rugby game. Come to think of it, I'm in favour of this kind of argument. It means words like discipline, commitment, perseverance and courage can all be left on the side, for I sense my genes liberating me from such archaic concepts. Even the study of wisdom or foolishness is merely describing what is, and can never change what isn't.

The more one begins to think this way, the more the fallacy becomes obvious. A recent cartoon in Newsweek took this logic further. The picture showed a scientist rushing into a room full of his co-workers grouped around a microscope. 'Eureka!' he exclaimed. 'I've discovered the gene that makes us think that everything's determined by genes!'

Our nature does affect who we are. How could it do otherwise? Yet there is more to us than chemistry and, although genetics may speak to us via our feelings, to use them as our guide or our god is a tragic mistake of epic proportions. There may be nothing between Brooke Shields and her Calvin Kleins, but thank God there is a whole lot between us and our genes!

3. Circumstances

Much has been written on this particular substitute for responsibility. Zig Ziglar wrote at length, in his bestselling book 'See You at the Top', on the concept of loser's limps. That is, the tendency we all have to blame external circumstance for internal condition. These excuses to fail come in many and varied form: our upbringing, culture, colour, parentage, our lack or abundance of education, our height, size, beauty or ugliness. Anything can be used as an explanation to why we have not or will not achieve. Yet one of the most outstanding similarities that the majority of successful people share, as evidenced in various studies, is that they all have had major obstacles to overcome. In other words, environment or circumstance for them were more adverse than the average.

It seems that if the context of one's life is contrary, one can respond by either becoming a victim or by reaching deep into the heart and finding the necessary resources to overcome. Shakespeare had Hamlet make this point:

'Whether tis nobler in the mind to suffer the slings and arrows of outrageous fortune or to take arms against a sea of troubles and by opposing, end them.'[1]

Our environment is not us, the frame is not the picture, the table setting is not the food, and the screen is not the image. Life may have handed us nothing but pain, but, as Helen Keller found out, pain may prove to be a microphone that enables us to reach the world. In that knowledge we discover that our hurt diminishes as we play our part in diminishing it in the lives of others. Our hearts interpret our circumstances and can make a heaven out of hell or a hell out of heaven.

4. Fatalism

Fatalism carries one of the most depressing messages there is. If you're going to hang, you're not going to drown. No matter what you do or don't do, the results will remain the same. My attainment of wisdom or not is purely up to the giant hand in the sky, spirit of the cosmos, or the way of the world. Call it Gaia or Vishnu, Jehovah or 'the force', somebody out there somewhere is watching and controlling us. Free will is merely illusionary. Most people, however, don't buy into this completely. It is not uncommon to hear phrases like, 'It was meant to happen,' or, 'I guess things just weren't meant to be.' In other words, we adapt the philosophy of fatalism so that it affects the large things (marriage, success, premature death and the like) but choose not to apply it to the small things ('Can you pass the salt?', 'Let's go to the zoo today' and 'I think I will go to bed now.'). I have trouble with this. Either fatalism is true the whole way or not at all. If we are puppets, then why are we allowed to think for ourselves about anything?

In reality, those who hold to these views, more often than not, do not do so out of firm conviction, but out of convenience or superstition. When things don't work out I can easily blame fate, and so I am off the hook. Thus we avoid the responsibility of our actions and, so the theory goes, become free and happy. Yet, freedom from responsibility is not true freedom. The lion in the cage may be free from the worry of where the next meal will come from, or whether he will survive the drought. He is released from the burden of choice that is involved in planning his day. Yet such responsibilities are the stuff of freedom. Those who choose to escape these demands simply become the most bound of all.

In the same way as the lion is designed for the sweeping plains, and the bird to fly across the expanse of the wide horizon, so we have been designed to live and to choose. With this comes both the potential for right choice and the potential for wrong. We have the ability to sense pleasure, but also to feel pain. The truth is we cannot have one without the other. Probably Shackleton, after his expeditions in Antarctica, put this best:

'In memories we are rich. We had pierced the veneer of outside things. We had suffered, starved and triumphed, grovelled yet grasped at glory, grown bigger in the bigness of life. We had seen God in his splendours, heard the text that nature renders. We had reached the naked soul of man.'

Love is not possible in a world where acceptance and compassion is automatic. Forgiveness means nothing if I don't have the choice not to forgive. I can only sense the wonder of joy because I have experienced the depths of tragedy. All too often we want the sweet without the sour, interaction without contradiction, faith without doubt, and victory without the fight. If that kind of world could have been possible, or is out there somewhere waiting for us to discover it, then I'm not sure that I would want to go. This life may be tough, but it is certainly better than all the alternatives I can think of.

5. Luck

I'm not sure whether the concept of being lucky or unlucky is a variant of fatalism, or if fatalism is a variant of luck. Either way both are used to escape the consequence of actions, or to negate blame. I am not saying that there is no such thing as luck, any more than I have suggested there is no such thing as God, circumstances, genetics or fate. (Well, actually I am saying there is no such thing as fate!) The question is whether luck is the sole, major or minor dispenser of what we find life delivering to us.

Most would agree it plays a part in the game of life. 'The harder I practice the luckier I get,' is true and not just of golf. Yet to gamble our future on luck or fate is to give away the gift of responsibility and therefore to exist disillusioned and disempowered.

So then, we are on our own. Left to face the music without the comfort or luxury of being able to point our fingers at other people or forces. This naked stage must become our home. We must be our own prompt and critic. Others will be there when the time is right, but they are not there to live our life or take the brunt of our bitterness. This is what growing up is all about.

Thus, the wisdom of responsibility is both self-admonishing and self-correcting and without it we are merely victims in a world that is unfair and doesn't care.

ENDNOTES

1   Shakespeare, *Hamlet*, Act 3, Scene 1.
2   As told in John Carmody, *How to Handle Trouble*,
    Doubleday, New York, 1993, p 14.
3   Zeus, 'When It Is Through Blindness...' *Odyssey*, Book One,
    30, as quoted by Barbara Tuchman, *The March of Folly*,
    Abacus, London, 1984, p 55.

Chapter 6

FUTURE CONSCIOUS

The Wisdom of Foresight

'Don't stop thinking about tomorrow,'

would have to be Fleetwood Mac's greatest, and maybe only, contribution to wisdom lore. Considering the future is one of the habits of the wise. I do not mean the sort of hazy dreaming of those who spend their waking moments exploring the fantasy kingdom of tomorrow-land. Such activity tends to be nothing more than escapism. Some escape forward and others backward into the equally surreal world of nostalgia and selective memory. The 'good old days' never were. Joy and pain tend to be recurring themes broken up into past, present and future. The wise hearted are not running from the now. They simply have a well developed perspective of time that is yet to be lived. Consequences of present action are thought through and considered and, as a result, decisions and activities tend to build the life rather than destroy it. The old adage puts it well: 'Fools run in where angels fear to tread.'

Wisdom declares that actions have consequences, choices have implications and lifestyle can lead to regret or reward. We are all acquainted with this truth. The wise, however, fine tune this knowledge into the discipline of discretion. They develop the habit of not moving forward until they have considered, as far as it is possible, where the path leads. This idea goes contrary to popular culture: 'Seize the day', 'Enjoy the moment', 'Follow your feelings' are the catch cries of our age and there is something within us all that wants to cast caution aside and place all our chips on the spinning roulette wheel of today.

Yet feelings cannot be allowed to dictate direction. Feelings are the froth and bubble of life. They are enjoyable and wonderful, yet they should not be the basis of our decision-making. Feelings are not a sign of truth. Yet masquerading for truth is what they do best for they speak loudly and convincingly, and we are easily seduced.

A friend of mine recently walked out on his wife and children because he felt like it. 'I feel free and happy, I know this is the right choice for me.' Unfortunately, experience shows that such a framework for decision-making is like building on quicksand. The foundations shift and a couple of years, or even months, down the track, life is filled with remorse and regret. The wise of heart, on the other hand, are governed by commitment, loyalty, love and honesty. Building on these things does not mean we escape the winters of life. We will still want, on occasion, to run and hide. But wisdom keeps us in the game so that our life will be held on course and, as a result, long-term meaning and fulfilment will be our reward.

Wisdom then always has an eye to the future, realising that one cannot break moral or spiritual law. We can run but we can't hide. We can avoid and ignore, but finally we discover that laziness leads to poverty, that industriousness and diligence lead to fulfilment and prosperity, that lust leads to disappointment, and love and commitment to real joy. Waiting for experience to teach us these lessons may be to wait too long. As one wit observed:

> *'Experience is the comb life gives us after*
> *we've lost our hair!'*

Sometimes I wish it were not so. The easy way, the instant way, is so much more attractive. We all want to lose weight without dieting, and get fit without exercising. We long to be proficient without study, and excellent without hard work. We want great marriages without effort, and successful businesses without the hard slog. In short, we want to live admirable and fulfiling lives without plumbing the depths of character, spirituality and self-sacrifice. My daughter wants to play her violin well without practice, and I would like to write books easily without thinking. Alas, the way of the world is not so. Treasure must be searched for, and character and greatness are never easy quarry. They are not captured by accident or luck. They must be pursued and, as we pursue, we discover that the chase is all part of the growing and the learning.

Solomon, when asked by God what he would like to receive, asked for wisdom. His choice shows that the seeds of wisdom were already planted within him. His choice was made not on what would benefit him in the moment, but what would be best over the long term. The gift of wisdom will finally bring to its owner everything else that is required for life. To realise this early on and to set one's target as wisdom, rather than money, prestige or personal happiness, is wisdom indeed. The Book of Proverbs puts it this way:

'The beginning of wisdom is... Get wisdom.'[1]

Thinking through the implications of present action is a little like playing chess. The best players are always four or five moves ahead, whereas I am happy if I move the piece correctly! What boggles the mind of many young chess players is the exponential growth of options as one moves into possible future board positions. Life, however, is not quite so complex. Normally each choice has several ramifications and, although we can never insure against the unusual or the unique, we can normally, if we give it the time and effort, work out what the future is more likely to be, given a certain course of action. If I choose to go to bed at two in the morning I will probably be tired when I have to wake up at seven. If I choose to avoid the growing relational problem at the office, it will probably turn into something far larger, rather than simply go away. If I have that other chocolate mousse... I will really enjoy it! Such a process can become more complex the further we look into the future.

Yet look we must, for the larger the decision, the more its impact, the larger the splash, the further the ripples extend. We can only see so far. The point is we are looking. Often the haze that is caused by the possible reactions of others, or a changing market, can obscure clear sight. But wisdom is not so much found in seeing the other shore, but in the willingness to peer over the side and navigate with the future in mind. This kind of approach will certainly minimise much of our self-inflicted pain.

I always remember the scene from the movie 'Fatal Attraction.' The husband, a character played by Michael Douglas, has just had a one-night affair and now, due to his lover's obsessiveness, realises he has to tell his wife. Her reaction is first stunned silence, then angry shouting as he tries to console her. Suddenly they are both aware of someone else in the room. They turn to see their young five-year-old son with a look of dismay and confusion, clutching his teddy bear. If Michael Douglas had thought through the implications of his actions, then I am sure the lustful gaze of Glenn Close would not have been so beguiling.

So, allowing things to simply take their course, allowing chemistry to obscure reality is nothing more than moral myopia. We all recognise the foolishness of choosing a moment of pleasure over a lifetime of happiness. The point is that normally such choices are not made. Things just get out of hand. We become so enamoured by the present moment that the future doesn't even get a glance... that is, until we are surrounded by it. I like what Charles Kettering once said:

> *'I spend most of my time thinking about the future because that is where I am going to spend the rest of my life.'*

The concept of future awareness is all about better decision-making and action. There are many who follow Kettering's advice, but their thoughts are not proactive, but reactive. We call this kind of activity 'worry' and, although it is mainly concerned with what may happen in the future, its energy hinders rather than helps. This is a result of several factors.

First of all, worry thinks on the worst possible scenario and, as a result, is rarely realistic. Probably ninety percent of what we are worrying about never happens. Secondly, worry tends to focus on that which we cannot change. Interest rates might go up, retrenchments may increase, rain may or may not come, our football team will probably not win, and on and on the list can go. Thirdly, the stuff of worry is not solution conscious. It is not about mapping out a preferable future, or changing events so as to diminish risk. No, because it focuses on that which is beyond control, its energy cannot be utilised on creative change.

There is, therefore, nowhere else for its current to flow except into the life of its bearer. This in turn can cause what we recognise as the many and varied symptoms of stress, from strokes to sweaty palms, from ulcers to aggression, from blood-pressure to bingeing. The outworking of nervous energy is a major cause of both crime and chronic illness.

Foresight and wise discretion are nothing like this, for their energy works toward answers, their owners are buoyed by their presence, and this aspect of wisdom helps move them towards a preferable future.

ENDNOTES

1   Proverbs 4:5.

Chapter 7

THINKING

The Wisdom of Concentration

'He that cannot reason is a fool, he that will not is a bigot, he that dare not is a slave.'

Anonymous

'I thought about it all the time.'

Sir Isaac Newton on how he discovered the law of gravity.

Thinking is both a source and a fruit of wisdom. Great men and women throughout history have often pointed out the fact that they were no different from others, save for one thing. They gave time and energy to thought. Alexander Hamilton put it this way: 'Men give me credit for some genius. All the genius I have is this. When I have a subject in mind, I study it profoundly. Day and night it is before me. My mind becomes pervaded with it... The effort which I have made is what people are pleased to call the fruit of genius. It is the fruit of labour and thought.'

Victor Hugo, the famous French novelist, said:

'Most people think once or twice in their lifetime. The reason that I have been successful is that I think once or twice a year!'

Our minds are God-given but like most gifts from above, only develop with use. This is why many do not reach anywhere near their potential. They use their brain not to create what isn't but to describe what is. The mind is reduced to simply being our personal commentator on life, analysing the plays, describing the action, but with no power to influence the game itself. We pick up habits from those around us, doing what others do, thinking what others think. Our minds can float with the stream and are never really stretched or challenged. Yet wisdom demands that the power of thought be released in our life. We must, in the words of Virginia Woolf:

'Think against the current, not with it'.

Then, and only then, will we know what we know.

As a pastor, one of the things that saddens me greatly is that many Christians know what they believe, but not why they believe it. They have accepted creed without criticism and thus when things go awry they can quickly let go from what appeared from the outside as heartfelt conviction. Faith is faith and is, by definition, something that goes beyond the observable, yet it should not go against reason. It is arational rather than irrational. Reason may tell us, courtesy of the Anthropic Principle, that this world is uniquely crafted for humanity and that belief in God is something that makes good sense of what we see and experience. Yet, whether we take this step of faith or not, whether we are theists, humanists or atheists, we should not hold our views out of prejudice, reaction or simply desire. In this way the honest and thinking Christian, or for that matter, atheist, holds their position not because they dislike the other positions or are making a statement against the values of parents or culture, or because they do not like the implications of the life change or the meaninglessness of the alternative view. No, they choose to believe or not to believe because of a desire for truth. Truth then, is the issue, and its shoulders can bear both investigation and criticism.

Hard-held conviction, when it has been inherited rather than arrived at, cannot handle open minded discussion. Thus, the atheist and the Christian who are so unthinkingly, can quickly become enraged and try to convince with emotional blackmail or outright force. Yet those who have the same views, but came by them honestly, so to speak, welcome discussion and are open to new ideas. I am not discounting faith. For me it is vital if one wants to connect with God and discover His grace. Yet, I recognise that clearheaded intention and heartfelt faith must walk together hand-in-hand for trust to be genuine.

HOW THINK YE?

It is one think to recognise the necessity for thought. It is something else again to begin to think both proactively and effectively.

Simply knowing the need does not produce the skill, and the skill of thinking is what is required. If you are anything like me, no sooner have I begun to think than a thousand other things come flooding into my mind. All trivial and yet almost overwhelming in their intensity.

'Where did I put that American Express card?', 'Did I turn the iron off?', 'Will the team win this weekend?', 'Do I need a hair cut?'. On and on it goes until the original big idea has been totally overrun. As Gulliver was entwined by the Lilliputians, so my own mind conspires against me.

After several years of wrestling so, I have come to the conclusion that it is all a plot. A plot hatched by my lazy cortex. This we must understand: all brains are stubbornly idle. They will only do what is required. They insist that their software is not right for exertion. They try to convince us we cannot, and since we are trained to believe our own heads, we do not.

I like Zig Ziglar's suggestion, that we would all be a bit better off if we were born without this particular organ and spent the first twenty-five years of our life saving so we could go out and buy one. After handing over the cash we would then receive this new accessory complete with owner's manual. 'Brains throughout history have learnt foreign languages, mastered

Algebra and become proficient in countless tasks from piano playing to polo,' states the guarantee.

So with zeal and expectation we would go to work and, due to our large investment, would not take the lame excuses for non-production that our new minds would proffer. We would not take no for an answer and, with both the will and the patience would discover slowly, but surely, our brains beginning to think and then to revel in this new discipline.

So how does one go about developing the habit of thought? The following are a few of the elements necessary for effective contemplation.

1. Be Intentional

'I went to the woods, because I wished to live deliberately, to front only the essential facts of life to see if I could learn what it had to teach, and not, when I came to die, discover that I had not lived...'[1]
Henry David Thoreau

In order to live deliberately, one must think deliberately. We do not think by mistake, it has to be done on purpose. It must be given time and space. The phrase, 'I'm going out to think,' is rarely heard these days. Yet one must treat this aspect of wisdom as seriously as a visit to the gym or the daily brushing of teeth. The cranium must be exercised. It must be asked questions that it does not know and then it must be made to ponder.

One of my friends has a thinking chair. Others go away to pray and to think for a couple of days a month. Such an on-purpose attitude will bring to its owner much reward, for the examined life is one that is never taken for granted and one that is experienced to the full.

2. Be Focused

The exclusion of mental chatter, so that one can concentrate on the issue at hand, tends to be a difficult skill to learn.

The eastern view of meditation is to empty the mind, to clean the slate, as it were, so that peace is reached and inner silence holds sway. An empty head may bring bliss for a while but it does nothing to actively change a life or influence a world. The brain is not designed to do nothing, but to do the right thing. The ancient Hebrew definition of meditation has this concept in mind. The word meant to muse, mutter and contemplate. It means to focus one's mind on a theme, problem or issue and then to go to work and think on it. It was G.K. Chesterton who said: 'An open mind is well and good, but like an open mouth its only purpose is to find something solid and nourishing, and then close upon it'.

3. Be Persistent

We began this chapter with a quote from Sir Isaac Newton that exemplifies this trait of effective thought. We must be intentional. We must be focused and then we must stay with it. The word meditation also carries with it the idea of chewing over, as the cow does the cud. Musing and ruminating are things not quickly done. Our rushed society does not lend itself well to such an exercise. The issue or problem may appear unsolvable and yet, given time, sometimes slowly and sometimes suddenly, but always wonderfully, answers will come.

How this happens, I do not know, but when we finally get our brains working and they figure out what we are trying to do, then night and day they keep at it. It is not unusual to hear of people receiving solutions to long mused over questions in the middle of the night, or when they first wake up. The subconscious and the conscious work together, and often the difference between a breakthrough or a fresh insight is simply another day, another month, even another year of intentional and focused thought.

This simple aphorism encapsulates the power of thought:

> 'You are not what you think you are, but what you think, you are.'

James Allen put it this way: 'A man is literally what he thinks, his character being the complete sum of all his thoughts.'[2]

Descartes insisted that: 'It is not enough to have a good mind, the main thing is to use it well.'[3]

The process of thought is involuntary, but the skill of thinking has to be worked on. Like any skill it gets better with practice. The more one thinks, the more one is able to. Yet in the same way an accomplished athlete reaches exhaustion, so the head can hurt and the brain go numb. Actually, I'm at this stage now. I have been able to get away for four days for the sole purpose of writing. Now, half-way through, my fingers are blistering but, worse than that, my mind is seizing. I am not sure if good wine or caffeine will get the thoughts flowing again or ring the death knell to today's mental activity, but at this stage I am willing to give anything a go!

Why is it so hard? Why can't the brain just produce on cue? Why does it have to be forced, word by painful word, fighting every phrase of the way? Yet think we must, regardless of our endeavour. Indeed, the failure to think is one of our world's greatest tragedies. Author Scott Peck goes as far as to say that thinking is the key to our existence. In this he is echoing Descartes' famous observation:

'Cognito ergo suma. I think, therefore I am.'

Today it seems many 'are not.' If existence is defined by the power and the process of the individual's thought life then, in this present era, we have countless multitudes who are not participating in the journey that is life. We have brains, we can think for ourselves, yet the pressure and the conditioning of society keeps people on a few limited and well used neural pathways. Thus, we are forced to allow everyone else to think in our place. Life has become a cliché. This is clearly evidenced by the incredible deterioration of creativity as people grow older. Some five percent of adults show a flair for creative thought. The percentage grows very slowly as we move down the age profile, until the age of five when it soars to over sixty percent! Creativity, it seems, is stymied when we go to school. Not because suddenly we have less input or mental stimulation, for this is clearly not the case. But by the sudden introduction of peer pressure and rules. The concept of colouring inside the lines, for example, is suddenly mandatory, and free expression is absorbed by class norm.

Yet let us not blame the individuals, it is the way of the world. By the time we reach adulthood, you would think we would have learnt. Unfortunately no. The cult, the culture, the company, all exert a pressure to conform which is hard to resist. It is only when we take a step away and look back do we ask ourselves that all too familiar question, 'What in the world was I thinking?' This realisation comes to us quickly when we are outside the group. From within, the view is different. That which appeared clever, and sophisticated, is often just foolishness when put into its wider context.

A few months back a certain trade union movement in my home city of Perth decided that the best way to highlight its concerns was to drive up one of our main freeways at a crawl during rush hour. Their vehicles blocked all lanes, and frustrated drivers were backed up for miles. What is astounding is that this group's industry had nothing to do with transport. They merely chose this form of protest to gain media exposure. For success to be theirs, they needed public

88

support. Yet that had been evaporated by the careful-
ly styled but stupid stunt. What were they thinking?
Well, the truth is, they probably thought it was a
good idea and, together between nods and beers,
they tied their collective noose.

The religious parents who try to control the thinking of their children rather than encouraging honest
investigation repel rather than attract the loyalty of
their child. The pastor, political leader or company
director who try to tell everyone what they must and
must not think is in danger of creating the very scenario they are trying to avoid.

We are, you see, designed to think, to investigate,
and to nut things out... When we are told not to, it
inspires. Yet when we finally realise we can, we don't.
We settle into suburbia and allow our minds to grow
muddy as we feed them on a constant diet of tabloid
journalism, soccer and soap opera. So, trashy paper-
backs sell well, songs like 'Achey Breaky Heart' make
it to number one, and the Spice Girls or sports stars
become our heroes. People are famous, and honoured simply because they are famous. Image is what
matters and the cash goes to those who entertain and
dull our minds rather than to those who provoke
them. What Randolph Bourne observed many years
ago is true today: 'Few people ever scratch the surface,
much less exhaust the contemplation of their own
experience.'[4]

Wisdom, then, is seen in the discipline of practised
thought which is not measured simply by quantity. It
is the quality and soundness of the activity which is

the gauge of productivity here. As Chamfort pointed out:

'A man is not necessarily intelligent because he has plenty of ideas anymore than he is a good general because he has plenty of soldiers.'[5]

Humans are the only thinking creatures. Not to use this remarkable function is to lower ourselves to a level which we were never meant to operate on.

ENDNOTES

1   Henry Thoreau, Walden, *The Portable Thoreau*, Penguin, New York, 1982, p 343.

2   James Allen, *As a Man Thinketh*, L.N. Fowler and Co., London, p 1.

3   Descartes, *Discourse on Method*, 1637.

4   Randolph Bourne, *Youth and Life*, 1913.

5   Chamfort, *Maximes et Pensees*, 1805.

Chapter 8

DISCIPLINE

The Wisdom of Restraint

'Think of your mind as a reservoir in which you have been storing up potential power... learning how to release that power in precise quantities and specific directions. This is the essence of self-discipline.'[1]

To be perfectly frank with you, the idea of discipline leaves me kind of cold. In short, I don't like it. It may be because of its association with going to the headmaster's office, something I had the privilege of doing on a number of occasions back in the good old days of corporal punishment! Boarding school at that time in England required the boys to be disciplined. Up at 6:50am, beds made by 7:15am. The day was thus scheduled until 8:30pm and lights out. The time and content of the meals were similarly organised: rice puddings on Tuesdays (make sure you avoid the skin), fish and chips on Fridays, the highlight of the week (sometimes you even got more than one chip!), lukewarm tapioca on Mondays, and roast beef for Sunday lunch (would you like one or two slices of gravy with that?). As a result, now some twenty years later, I still cannot stomach such things as custard or porridge... the memory of those lumps still linger!

What has all this to do with discipline? Not much, but it has given me the opportunity to share a little of my abused childhood! But as a result of all this, I hope you can understand why the 'D' word is not one of my favourites. Discipline, for many of us, has received bad press. Yet the wisdom would quickly dismiss such adolescent or childhood phobias and insist we investigate, develop and utilise this much-needed aspect of wise living. Without its strength we stand little chance of reaching our goals or running our lives.

Author Scott Peck defines discipline as the act of 'scheduling the pain and pleasure in life'. Confronting painful things first and allowing pleasure to follow on is not the natural way to live, yet it is the wise way to live, for life is tough and hard decisions need to be made. Discipline allows us to so control our actions and emotions. It holds us back from running off at the mouth when provoked or plunging into disillusionment or despair when things don't work out our way. In short, self-discipline keeps us accountable to God, friends and family as well as our own destinies, dreams and deep desires. Let us look, then, at a couple of the applications of self-discipline.

1. Preparational Discipline

The great difference between achieving and activity is the discipline of preparation.

I have always been fascinated by the skyscraper. I remember when a fifty-five storey building was begun in Perth. In the months that followed I grew increasingly frustrated as it seemed no progress was being made. I quickly came to understand that any high building, great endeavour, or extraordinary life needs time to develop. Foundations must be laid. Unseen work must be carried out. For then, and only then, can the building or life rise to dwarf those around them. Proper preparation determines potential.

Planning, for many, is simply boring. We have this need to get on with the job. Somehow sitting, thinking, strategising and organising before the gun goes off feels like a waste of time. 'We must act', we declare. 'We musn't just sit and talk. This is no time for committee discussion. This is a time for doing. Some are in the ditch on the other side of the road where life is all talk and action is forgotten. The ongoing committee meeting in Monty Python's 'Life of Brian' is a wonderfully comic example of this. 'Now is not the time for endless chatter, now is a time for revolution... let us formulate a motion for immediate action...' and on and on the verbal meandering continues. The wise, however, are able to balance correctly the twin demands of preparation and action.

The apathetic and the fearful often need to be motivated to move, but for the average person the emphasis must be on giving due time and effort to preparation.

As Solomon states:

> 'The wise look ahead. The fool attempts to fool himself and won't face the facts.'[2]

Old steam trains work on the principle of energy and pressure being allowed to build up before the valves are opened. To try to release the energy too quickly generally results in premature recapitulation.

Unfortunately it seems to me that men suffer in this area the most. If I sound sexist it is to my own gender's detriment. My inclination is always to get up and go, and if we are on the move let's not stop, no matter what the reason.

Driving is a good example of this. Time taken to read the map pays off in the long run but I often am too stubborn for that. 'Let's keep going, we will recognise something soon! We may be lost but at least we are making good time!'

In the same manner, lack of planning can cause our lives to reach an unexpected and unwanted place. We pretend we actually purposed to be where we are but inwardly we are berating ourselves for lack of forethought.

It is all a little bit like the Charlie Brown cartoon where Charlie is busily painting a target around his wall-stuck arrow. In response to Lucy's question of, 'Why?', he merely retorts, 'This way I never miss!'

Thus, without preparation, the disorganised soul is blown with the wind and cannot then be picky about the direction or destination.

2. Emotional Discipline

Emotional control is as difficult as it is essential. Now, I must be careful not to give the wrong impression. Mr Spock here is as much out of line as those whose lives are governed solely by the sensory. Emotions are not designed to be our guide, or our ultimate counsellor. The person who cannot show emotion, or who feels that to do so is inherently weak, is as unhealthy as the individual whose emotions have taken the place of their personality. When loved ones die we grieve, when sun sparkles on snow we smile, when children are born we dance and when hopes are dashed we cry. The laughter of love and the grimace of pain authenticate our journey and help us deal with the process of life.

In fact, emotions enhance the experience. Through them we participate in the story. Do I laugh at a joke because it's funny, or is it funny because I laugh? The applause at the end of a performance doesn't just appreciate but adds to the experience as well. The quiet, cold spectator is just an observer, but is not alive in the true sense of the word. This is why, when things are happening, people respond emotionally. If I preach a good sermon I want to hear congregational response, not because my ego needs the affirmation of the applause or nods of agreement, but because it shows that we are alive. We are participating together. In our church people can also express disappointment and disagreement by hissing. But, of course, I never say anything that could be deemed as hissable!... (That normally gets a loud one!)

The world has recently seen an incredible release of feeling from that most conservative of nations, England. With the passing of Diana, Princess of Wales, a powerful surge of emotion swept across the world. The catharsis was healthy. It helped people come to terms with what had happened and was as appropriate as it was needed. Yet even within this atmosphere there were those who tried to raise their voice against such feeling. This cold and narrow intelligentsia would rather people behave themselves in public and shed a tear or two in the privacy of their own homes. As one writer to Time magazine, responding to this attitude correctly asks, 'Do we really want to know what the wave of emotions over Princess Diana's death means? Do we really need analysts to explain sadness and define guilt for us? There are times... when it is enough just to feel.'[3] The grey and dispassionate world of the non-feeling and cynical is not a sign of their superior life; merely a sign that they are closer to death than everyone else.

So, emotions help us celebrate life and adapt to loss. Yet when we expand their job description to include key decisions in areas like marriage or divorce, work or worship, we find that they have reached their level of incompetence. Emotions are not designed to call the shots. The cheering (or hissing) audiences are not there to write the speech. Our taste buds are meant to savour the food, not write the recipe or cook the meal. When life is lived upon the basis of feeling, then disillusionment and self-destruction become our lot.

There seems to be no clever strategy or universally effective formula that one could follow in order to keep emotions in their proper place. Such detail we normally have to work out for ourselves.

What seems to be the most important key is simply the truth that we have been discussing. Namely, that emotions are wonderful, but we must not take our orders from them. In an age where there is a vacuum of morals and absolutes, such a statement seems revolutionary to some. 'Where else should I turn, if not to my feelings?' Will and Ariel Durant encapsulated the state of our age well when they wrote:

'Caught in the relaxing interval between one moral code and the next, an unlawed generation surrenders itself to luxury, corruption, and a restless disorder of family and morals.'[4]

It is the instructed heart that is wise, not the goosebump. Wisdom would have us live from within rather than from without. Those who live by feelings are at the whim and control of circumstance, but the wise heart helps to interpret the life, enabling us to choose between the myriad of pathways.

3. The Discipline of Appetite

This aspect of self-discipline is probably the most familiar. More books and articles have been written about it than almost anything else that we will discuss in this volume. The fact that self-discipline must extend to the areas of food intake, alcohol consumption and sexual activity, are reasonably self-evident. Some choose to control these appetites by, as far as it is possible, curtailing them completely. The tee-totaller and the celibate have chosen this path. It is a little harder to apply this strategy to the area of food! These appetites are God-given, but they cannot be allowed to rule. Eating is different from gluttony, drinking from drunkenness, and making love from having sex. Our body always wants more, for pleasure proves addictive. Yet pleasure, and not hedonism, is legitimate. Life spent in a Hefner-style dressing gown is as meaningless as it is unfulfilling. As someone once said, 'The best argument against a life devoted to pleasure is found in the attempt to live it.'

One of the reasons the book of Ecclesiastes is included in the canon of Scripture is that it makes this point very well. Solomon fulfiled all his appetites, and he fulfiled them absolutely, for he had the wherewithal to do it. The appetite for sex was explored with the cooperation and participation of 'seven hundred wives and three hundred concubines.'[5] He built splendid palaces, amassed great fortunes... and his conclusions, 'I denied myself nothing my eyes desired; I refused my heart no pleasure. My heart took delight in all my work, and this was the reward for all my labour. Yet when I surveyed all that my hands had done and what I had toiled to achieve, everything was meaningless, a chasing after the wind.'[6]

Appetites are harsh task masters and lousy gods. Many a life has been wasted as this conclusion of Solomon is finally reached, but by then it is all too late. Wisdom and self-discipline would encourage us to learn these lessons now, before our time is gone.

I wrote in a previous book, 'Secrets of Super Achievers', about the characteristic of discipline. It is, of course, one of the foremost secrets of those who achieve in life. Part of that book is worth repeating here for it is pertinent to the developing of this aspect of wisdom in our lives.

Discipline, I have discovered, has an intrinsic ability to be self-perpetuating. The individual whose life is totally lacking in it need only concentrate on one area of his behaviour. It matters not what habit one chooses to reform: diet, exercise, sleeping schedule or punctuality. For when discipline begins in the corner of one's existence it will begin to grow, reproduce itself and breed. A sort of momentum takes over and our disorganised private world, much to our delight and surprise, is quietly conquered. It is character's version of the domino theory. Yet the process must be started and much energy expended in the first month in developing a discipline. Then energy and resolve are produced from this one area, enough to continue and more besides. On the other hand, once there is a break in the pattern, once we allow discouragement, laziness, or even a simple holiday, to erode these now well-cemented habits, momentum dies and entropy sets in.

The reason most die with their music still in them is they presume upon talent and expect gifting to create success. This philosophy of life gradually gives rise to a disappointment-driven melancholy which will eventually permeate every moment of the day. The loss of discipline will always signal the death of a dream. Enthusiam and passion have their time, they belong to the race at it's beginning and at it's end, when the applause of the crowd can be heard. Yet for the bulk of the race it is the steady steps, mile after mile, unseen and unappreciated, when discipline comes to the fore.[7]

ENDNOTES

1 *Napoleon Hill's Keys to Success*, Editor - Matthew Sartwell, Paitkus, London, 1994, p 108.

2 Proverbs 13:16.

3 Vardit Koroth, Time, October 13th 1997, p 8.

4 As quoted, Harpers, August 1997, p 35.

5 1 Kings 11:3.

6 Ecclesiastes 2:10 & 11.

7 Philip Baker, *Secrets of Super Achievers*, Webb & Partners, Perth, 1997. p 147, 153.

Chapter 9

TEACHABILITY

The Wisdom of Curiosity

'I fancy many would have arrived at wisdom if they had not fancied they had already arrived.'[1]

The furnace of wisdom needs constant feeding. Input precedes output. Facts, observations, feelings and information are all digested. Together they produce the fuel necessary to power the wise heart. Thus, one of the key attributes of wisdom is this thing we call personal growth. Growth of the heart or the head, however, are not just means to an end. Scott Peck in his book, 'Further Along The Road Less Travelled' went as far as to define the meaning of life as personal progress. Not to grow, not to change, is to die. Sadly, many have passed on, long before burial. We know enough to survive, to do our job, and so we stagnate. To suddenly realise this can be as shocking as it is sad.

What works for us today may not work for us tomorrow, and if we don't make the effort to change and to learn, then regret will fill our latter years. Two stories spring to mind. The first concerns one individual who, when applying for a job which required greater seniority, responsibility and proficiency, had the phrase from their C.V., 'twenty years experience', fiercely debated. 'Explain to me how you've had twenty year's experience,' demanded the senior partner of the new company. 'From my understanding and from what you've said, all you've had is one year's experience repeated twenty times!'

The second illustration is from the documentary, 'Blue Eyed'. The programme features a feisty school teacher, Jane Elliot from Iowa, who, twenty years earlier, designed and initiated a bold experiment to communicate the evil of racism to her class of seven-year-olds. She segregated the class on eye colour and, for one day, the blue eyes were treated with absolute disdain, whilst the brown eyes ruled the roost. The situation was reversed the second day. The results were dramatic and astounding and had such an impact on the children, that many follow-up documentaries have been made.

The one I was watching showed Ms Elliot, now in her fifties, putting groups of primary and secondary school teachers through the same exercise. In the discussion afterwards one very pleasant Mid-Western girl in her late twenties, with blonde hair and sparkly eyes giggled as she talked about her feelings. She was very sweet as she pretended to be both comical and unperturbed by the experience she had just been through. Jane Elliot stood right in front of her, very seriously and impassively, until she had finished. Ms Elliott then pointed her finger in the young lady's face and said with great strength and passion, 'Can I tell you something, lady, can I tell you something that will help make a difference to your life over the next thirty years... get over cute! You're cute now and everyone thinks it's funny, but when you're forty-two you will just be another broad, and there will be a whole host of younger, sweeter things than you around that will take your job and win the superficial admiration of those around them. Get over cute, or you will be crying and complaining and blaming the world on why its turned against you. Get trained, get competent and grow up!' This left the young lady in tears, but I felt sure that the impact of such hard-hitting truth had made its mark.

Life is tough. To stay stationary is stupid. We are designed to grow, to progress, to be bigger people. The wise hearted relish the challenge and begin to look at how this essential task can be accomplished. The following are some of the ingredients necessary for accomplishing such inner growth.

1. Curiosity

The art of curiosity must be fanned white hot if one is to uncover the truth that surrounds us. The wise have always realised this and have nurtured their curiosity almost with religious respect. Listen to what Albert Einstein said concerning it:

'The important thing is not to stop questioning... never lose a holy curiosity.'

Or what John Locke, the English philosopher wrote: 'I attribute the little I know to my not having been ashamed to ask for information and to my... conversing with all descriptions of men on those topics that form their own peculiar professions and pursuits.' The desire to learn from each person that comes across our path is played out almost as a game. The opportunity is never lost to ask questions or to note observations.

George Herbert Palmer, the American educator stated:

'I am defeated, and know it, if I meet any human being from whom I find myself unable to learn anything.'

This attitude is extremely healthy. One of the dangers of a little knowledge is that it can masquerade as most knowledge. When we learn, we think we know, and the attribute of being teachable, which got us to where we were in the first place, begins to fade under the perceived brightness of our own brilliance. Even someone of the magnitude of Aristotle is not exempt. As Bertrand Russell once remarked:

'Aristotle could have avoided the mistake of thinking that women have fewer teeth than men by the simple device of asking Mrs Aristotle to open her mouth!'

Part of my role as the leader of a church is to attend Pastors and Ministers Seminars either as a speaker or a delegate. One can normally pick the 'most likely to succeed' men or women by both the quality and the quantity of questions asked. One young ministerial student in America wrote to every pastor he could find who had proved themselves highly effective. He asked for an appointment, and offered to pay for their time, merely to sit down and ask questions. These leaders all agreed and did not charge. The joy of teaching someone who wanted to learn will motivate any leader worth his salt. It is of no surprise the young man concerned, now pastors one of America's largest churches, with some fifteen thousand attending weekly. There are countless others who have not this curiosity who struggle on from week to week with either pride, apathy or cynicism, killing their curiosity and thus robbing them of the knowledge necessary to move ahead.

2. Unlearning

I used to think that sushi was sickening, that beaches were better than mountains, that Renault Dauphines were great cars and that Michael Bailey (the twelve-year-old in the next class) was a fast bowler. I used to think that Whangarei (population 35,000) was a big city and that Paris would be a horrible place to visit. I used to think Christians were always nice, and that non-Christians weren't, that life was pretty black and white and brussel sprouts weren't edible. I used to think that bungy-jumping was scary. I used to think a lot of things, but now I don't. I have learnt better (although I still think bungy-jumping is scary!). The point is, the process of learning necessarily means that along the road we not only acquire new information but have to jettison material as well. All of us leave in our wake the flotsam and jetsam of failed notion and outgrown theory.

The wise are willing to discard more than most. Pet theories or peer-held truths hold no special attachment. Once an error is seen, over the side it goes. The wise also vary from the norm in the analysis of what should or shouldn't go. Babies must not get thrown out with bath water, or messengers with messages. Everything should be judged on its own merits. The foolish don't so much unlearn as rearrange their ignorances.

Furthermore, the wise realise that nothing should be unlearned simply due to personal preference; many change their views simply because they want to disagree with parents or be accepted by friends. Wisdom doesn't run with the crowd. Athanasius clung to the doctrine of the Trinity when the tide of intellectual opinion had turned against it. Then he was noted as an heretic, now as a saviour of the truth. Yet wisdom doesn't just follow the minority. Ideas and convictions are not like fashion, where some purchase because everyone else does, whilst others prize individuality and uniqueness higher than wearing what they actually look good in. I must confess, I am amongst the latter group. Nothing annoys me more than to purchase a watch or buy a print only to discover that they have become 'in'. I mean, I may have started the trend, but now I am just one of the number. So away with ducks on the wall, fluffy dice hanging on my rear vision mirror, and bright coloured ties... one has to stay ahead of the pack! This is all well and good with art or attire, but the wells of truth, values and ideas cannot be treated with such disdain. The ability to discern what should be unlearned, and then the courage and humility to erase and record over, are the necessary qualities of those who would progress and grow.

3. Continued Desperation

When driving in America it takes me a couple of weeks to orientate myself to 'right-side of the road' travelling. I've noticed in such a transition there are several stages.

First of all, when you pull out onto the freeway in your new hire car, the awareness of your vulnerability and ignorance cause your concentration powers to be exercised to the full. In this first stage one never trusts one's feelings. To relax is to court disaster. Because the mental and physical habits of driving on the opposite side will quickly return and, as a result, scare the pants off you!

After several days, stage two is entered. You are halfway towards being fully American. The hand taps on the steering wheel in time to Achey Breaky Heart, you laugh at the antics of Rush Limbaugh or Howard Stern, and you stay on the correct side of the road without having to think about it... most of the time.

After several weeks in this in-between phase of dual nationality, you've finally arrived. In stage three you never look the wrong way to find your rear vision mirror, you can yell abuse and give the right culturally accepted physical gesture as well. In short, you have reprogrammed both your body and mind to think and drive on the right.

I put it to you that the most difficult and dangerous of these stages is stage number two. The temptation to relax increases, but at the point of crisis, one does not know whether to trust intuition. That impulse to pull the steering wheel to the left to get out of the way of the flashing blue lights. Is that the old me or the new me?! Tony Robbins compares this scenario to life. Those who are having a bad life will realise it and try everything to change it. Their desperation, like the concentration of the driver, is strong enough to produce change. However, when life is okay, when we are more happy than not or, to put it another way, when we are not unhappy, it becomes easy to throttle back on the desire for better things and settle in to what essentially is a half-way house.

The Bible speaks of being lukewarm as the most difficult place to be. The reason for this is self-evident. In stage one, our lack of happiness and our intense feelings of failure mean that only two courses of action are open to us. First, we can dig in and develop multiple defence mechanisms. Such a strategy will only turn our searchlight outward rather than inward. Pride, anger, and bitterness will then become our lot, as we live life as a victim. Or, we channel our desperation into the areas of new information and personal change and slowly find ourselves pulling out of the mire.

The lukewarm stage is dangerous because we have experienced just enough success to seriously inhibit, or even destroy, our openness to learn. It is here the wise one stokes up the fires, maintains the focus, fixes the eyes on the goal which is still ahead, and moves beyond the mediocrity of okay.

This phenomena is seen not only in individuals, but also in nations. Australia prides itself, in comparison to other countries, as being somewhere in the top ten or twenty, depending on what the variable is. Our politicians are quick to say that there is always someone worse than us. We in this land, however, should not compare ourselves with what others are doing, but rather compare ourselves to our own potential. We should make comparison, not with what has been, but what could be. When we limit ourselves to the 'already', we will never discover the 'not yet'. The plans and the blueprint of the 'not yet' are found only in the world of thinking, dreaming and creativity.

The only way to break out of stage two and into stage three is to begin to conquer this new territory, push out the boundaries of our life, and be satisfied with nothing less than what we were meant to be. Pastors of successful churches or C.E.O.s of booming companies will quickly fade when they consider themselves as successful. If we have 'arrived' then there is no impetus to continue the journey. Inner paralysis, even shrinkage, begins to take place, and the life, company or church will quickly lose their cutting edge. Movement from stage one to stage three will only occur if we are motivated by personal vision and a hunger for what could be. Unfortunately, we often get distracted and are tempted to settle for mediocrity. We sell our birthright for soup and lose sight of the beckoning horizon.

Not all spheres of life, however, operate this way. Take the example of physical conditioning. Three phases of fitness can clearly be seen: the unfit, the partly fit and the totally fit. Yet when one is totally fit, the emphasis is not on continued improvement but on maintaining the ground that has been taken. There is only so far one can go in this area of life. To push the boundaries could lead to excessive and compulsive behaviour and, in the process, harm the body. Yet the inner world has no such limits. There is always room for growth in the soul. Thus, the attitude of continuing; never-ending internal improvement is a fundamental attitude of wisdom.

This characteristic of teachability is a key on the road to wisdom. Yet teachability is not just about attitude but about action. One must not just be receptive to new information, one must also search for it. Truth lies often below the surface. It hides in unlikely places and is easily missed by those who rush for instant solutions. This quest, driven by desperation and fuelled by desire, is part of the journey towards wisdom. As we seek and strive, we grow. Wisdom hidden not from us but for us. Those who hyperplane through life, can never pick it up. Wisdom is simply too precious for that, it must be purchased by blood, sweat and tears. The willingness to pay such a price is, in itself, absolutely necessary to build the internal capacity to handle such wisdom when found.

Like the chick cracking through the egg, to offer help is to deprive the young life of the necessary struggle. Desperation and the fight to be born give the capacity for this new life to survive. Wisdom cannot be purchased secondhand. It must be appropriated the hard way. Not to wrestle so, we will only discover a surreal world of superficial clichés and philosophical dribble. A wisdom that is miles broad and inches deep, a wisdom that is book-generated rather than nourished by contemplation, a wisdom that finds its home in the memory banks rather than in the heart.

What actions, then, does this attitude of teachability prompt?

1. Asking the Right Questions

The ability to ask the right questions is crucial if one is to grow. Wisdom is found in other peoples lives. Getting at it is the key. The ancient Book of Proverbs speaks of wisdom being hidden deep within a person, but a person of understanding will be able to draw it out. The picture is one of a well, which contains clear and refreshing water. The thirsty will only drink from such a reservoir if they know how to draw the water up. So it is with wisdom.

I remember once watching an interview on New Zealand television. The interviewee was Norman

Vincent Peale. The right questions would have led to
a fascinating insight into such a man. Yet the inter-
viewer was young and inexperienced. Her whole
knowledge of Dr Peale derived from the short bio she
had quickly read ten minutes before, thus her opportunity, and ours, was wasted. We learnt of Dr Peale's
lack of rugby knowledge and his enjoyment of the
New Zealand countryside, but that was as far as
things went. The questions were banal and mundane
and I, the viewer, felt cheated.

So often we squander our opportunities by simply
not asking the right questions. A good question can
unlock the unconscious stream of thought and bring
long-hidden treasures to the surface.

2. Asking the Right People

It is not enough to ask the right questions. One
must ask the right people as well.

I am a lover of good coffee: latte, espresso, con
panna, macchiato. Many times in my travels I am in a
town or city wanting to know where the best coffee
is... I have the right question, but I must also ask the
right person. Not to do so will find me leaving all
over town, quarter-drunk mugs of instant imitations
of the real thing. One must find a coffee lover, and
they will know. The old Italian man will be more
helpful here than the Chinese immigrant. Different
cultures have their strengths. The Yugoslavs know little of sushi, while the Japanese seem to be ignorant
of the varieties of real ale available from Kentish

pubs. The English don't understand baseball, and the Americans... well, time and space does not allow me...! The moral of all this is that one must know whom to ask for what.

THE ULTIMATE QUESTIONS

The attitude of teachability is probably seen best in the big questions. To face them requires both courage and diligence; to pursue them, steadfastness and humility. The journey must be one that makes truth its destination rather than pleasure or happiness.

I've always thought the American Constitution gave too much emphasis to happiness. Now, I have no problem with its pursuit, but happiness is always the by-product of more lofty ideals. America itself was settled by those who knew this well. The Pilgrim Fathers found their purpose in the search for God and ultimate meaning. Whereas, south of the border, the Spanish came on a quest for gold and glory. I think that the campfires of the former echoed with more laughter than those of the latter. There would be little time amongst the counting of the coins to enjoy the sunsets or play with the kids.

The wise of heart thus realises that the quest for meaning is all important. To replace it with crass superficialities, such as happiness or cash, is self-deception in the extreme. How do we forget so soon the lessons of history and the morals of the old stories? I still hear, from time to time, the phrase, 'I wish

I had the Midas touch,' used with a tone of desire for what is not. Yet the point of the Midas story is that his touch destroyed him, everything became gold: food, water, loved ones... Strange how the image of Midas remains, yet the truth behind his tale is conveniently forgotten.

Our lives are not designed to simply be, to exist and float through time experiencing its varied feelings and frustrations. We cannot live without this thing we call meaning. We must have a purpose, there has to be a reason behind the journey. These are heavy and unquiet thoughts. Many choose not to pursue them for fear of what they may discover. Yet wisdom dictates that, if there is meaning, it must be found, if there is not, it must be faced. Os Guiness, writer, thinker and apologist, speaks of this quest and shows that most end up at either extreme of the meaning continuum. He calls one of these 'diversion'. This is where the fear of non-meaning, of discovering nothing or, even worse, discovering something, causes the unwise soul to divert their attention away from the probing questions. Thus the cricket or the football, the garden or the upcoming holiday become subjects that take on an almost religious fervour and devotion. The embroidery of life becomes central. These things may fill the void, in the same way as bread and butter will fill an empty stomach. Yet the sensation is transient and unfulfilling. There is behind it all a sense that something is not quite right, that maybe it doesn't really matter if the team wins or the roses bloom. Yet everyone else is cheering. Others are devoting their life to these things. The emperor may have no clothes on, but why point it out and ruin everyone's fun? After all, it may be just me. If I pretend longer, maybe the assurance will come, that this is what life is all about and then everything will be wonderful. Such diversion will quickly lead to a lethargy of life, a sort of walking, sleeping sickness where the days pass by and no-one seems to care.

The other extreme on Guiness' continuum he calls despair. This is where the decision is made to seek, but if the journey goes awry, if wrong conclusions are reached, then depression and disillusionment are the inevitable result. The rising suicide rate amongst our youth is one tragic sign that Os Guiness is correct.

Let me clarify what I mean by 'wrong conclusions'. I am, of course, speaking subjectively. Different conclusions will result in different interpretations of the world and our place within it. The conclusion of non-meaning is a difficult one to assimilate. If there is no God, then there is no ultimate meaning or absolutes. As one philosopher pointed out, 'If God is dead, then everything is permissible.' Such a statement is, of course, correct. Whether one follows humanism, hedonism or existentialism, it is all rearranging deck chairs on the Titanic. In the end everything is pointless. As we contemplate such things, I think we can see why the diversionary life is so appealing. Yet deep down we rage against this, we want to fight for meaning and trust that God is, and all is well. This very struggle does, in itself, point towards a way out of the maze.

C.S. Lewis put it far better than I could when he said:

'If the whole universe has no meaning, we should never have found out that it has no meaning: Just as, if there were no light in the universe and therefore no creatures with eyes, we should never know it was dark. 'Dark' would be a word without meaning.'

What Lewis is describing comes directly from his own experience. As an atheist his argument against God was that the universe seemed so cruel and unjust, but then, if this was indeed the case, why did he feel so? How had he come by the idea of just and unjust?

Lewis continues: 'A man does not call a line crooked unless he has some idea of a straight line. What was I comparing this universe with when I called it unjust? If the whole show was bad and senseless from A to Z, so to speak, why did I, who was supposed to be part of the show, find myself in such violent reaction against it? A man feels wet when he falls into water because man is not a water animal: A fish would not feel wet. Of course, I could have given up my idea of justice by saying that it was nothing but a private idea of my own, but if I did that then my argument against God collapsed too, for the argument depended on saying that the world was really unjust, not simply that it did not happen to please my fancies. Thus, in the very act of trying to prove that God did not exist, in other words that the whole of reality was senseless, I found I was forced to assume that one part of reality, namely my idea of justice, was full of sense. Consequently, atheism turns out to be too simple.'2

I have great respect for those who do not believe in God and do so honestly. I frequently write to one of Australia's leading atheists and find the discussion invigorating. His conclusions about life are different from mine, and he's valiantly attempting to live a purposeful life in a world of non-meaning. I, though, find my heart pulled in a different direction. I find solace in prayer and renewed vigour from ultimate hope. I believe what I believe, not out of a sense of avoiding the pain of the alternative, but from my limited observation of the world and the understanding of my own heart. I discover I have an instinct for immortality, a sense of right and wrong and a thirst for spiritual things which only makes sense if real life-giving water is available.

Wisdom, then, is seen more in the pursuit than in the conclusion, more in the quest than the destination. It refuses to be put off the investigation of such matters by the antics of religious fanaticism on the one hand, or the cerebral arrogance of the reactionary or embittered sceptic on the other. Wisdom simply realises that this is one journey it has to take. It must find meaning. It must find an anchor for the soul and a mooring for the heart. There must be a cause bigger than the individual into which one can sow one's life. For out of such a cause will flow fulfilment, happiness and peace, and without it self-

120

absorption or self-destruction will take precedence. When this is allowed to happen the once promising fruit of a worthwhile life will perish unsavoured and uneaten.

ENDNOTES

1   Seneca, *De tranquilitate Animi*: Chapter 1, Sec. 16.
2   C.S. Lewis, *Mere Christianity*, Collins, Glasgow, 1952,
      p 2.

Chapter 10

CUNNING

The Wisdom of Guile

The concept of cunning has a sort of mischievous ring to it. We tend to connect the word quite easily with criminals, rascals and shady entrepreneurs. Those who use their cunning to manipulate or connive seem to have hijacked the word to the degree that the phrase, 'He is a cunning individual,' is more pejorative than praise. Yet one of wisdom's aspects is this very attribute. Jesus spoke to his disciples regarding it. He encouraged them, that in their mission of communicating the gospel effectively to their generation and the generations to come they must be:

'Wise as serpents, harmless as doves.'[1]

Now, I am the first to admit that some of his followers in our day and age may have taken this concept to extremes! But the basic idea is sound. Street smarts, knowing how things are, shunning naivety and gullibility... these are the attributes of the cunning. Wisdom realises where it's at.

The cunning can differentiate between honesty and discretion. They know when to speak and when to be silent. They understand the use of buzz words and will change their vocabulary to connect with those they are trying to reach or relate to. The idealistic can often fail to be effective if they lack this vital ingredient. Refusing to budge on issues like dress or language under the name of 'not compromising my individuality' can result in missed opportunity or unnecessary offense. The heart of the wise will never compromise on values or beliefs, but is pliable in less significant areas. The cunning can roll with the punches, move with the times and adapt to changing circumstances.

Jesus was not the only one to use the nature of various animals to describe this particular aspect of wisdom. Niccolo Machiavelli in his best-known work, The Prince, uses the analogy of lions and foxes. He writes to potential rulers and political leaders on the correct application of both force and cunning.

'It is necessary for a prince to know how to use the animal, therefore, he should choose the fox and the lion from amongst their ranks. Since the lion cannot defend itself against traps and the fox cannot defend itself from the wolves. One needs to be a fox, therefore, to recognise traps, and a lion to frighten the wolves. Those who rely simply on the lion do not understand this.'[2]

I think Kennedy showed cunning when he refused to board Soviet vessels as they stopped at the blockade line outside of Cuba in 1962. He thus allowed Khrushchev to back down with grace. He gave him room to manoeuvre. So World War Three was averted whilst some American admirals quietly fumed due to their government's 'lack of resolve'. Foolishness often refuses to negotiate whilst wisdom is striking a deal. Foolishness makes a huge commotion over formulas yet fails to protect principles. The cunning on the other hand are happy to forsake a minor for the sake of a major. As William James said in his principles of psychology:

> *'The art of being wise is the art of knowing what to overlook.'*

I have seen those who quit their jobs over what is, in the final analysis, a technicality. Making a mountain out of a molehill, they fume and vent. Yet a few months down the track, when the dust has settled and focus has come to their vision, they regret their foolhardy actions. The cunning realise that there are several ways to skin a cat. They would probably make some money on the cat skin as well! They will quickly agree on price as long as they can set the terms. I mean, who wouldn't buy a million dollar house which is only worth $800 000 if the terms are $1 per year?!

The cunning have always had the edge throughout history. From the wooden horse of Troy to the bouncing bombs of the dam busters. The element of surprise and 'outthinking' the opposition are vital in war, sport or business. The winged keel of Australia II was the edge that finally wrested the America's Cup from the New York Yacht Club. Mohammed Ali's constant talk of dancing around his opponent, Joe Frasier, in the 'rumble in the jungle' was Ali at his best. When the fight came, Ali stood toe to toe and slugged it out. Frasier's camp was not ready for this. The psychological blow of misapplied preparation gave the challenger the upper hand and the championship was regained. All great leaders have exhibited this characteristic. Ghandi showed it in his demand to go to prison over the infringing of unjust laws. He knew that in so doing he would build support for his cause and show up the absurdity of the laws as well. Thatcher showed it in her firmness and zeal over the Falklands. She rode the wave of public support and legitimately used the emotion of the moment to guarantee another term in office. Vaclav Havel exemplified it when, in addressing the Czech people in his first major political speech, he pointed out that their problems must not be blamed on the external force of communism, but on their own lack of resolve and fortitude. Thus he focused the energy of the country on moving into the future together with hope, rather than becoming bitter and resentful, remaining the tragic victims of the past. Mandela and Churchill, Peron and Castro all have shown such smarts. They all have this cunning streak, and over and over again it has proved to be their making.

I believe it requires great cunning to raise teenagers successfully, to win at cards without cheating, and to watch what you want on television without annoying your wife! The wisdom can be wiley. Indeed, in this day and age, it is not an option. To win in life, one must stay ahead of the play. Whether you are trying to catch a trout or an overbooked flight, buying a house or haggling for a bargain, this attribute of wisdom is an essential ally. Those who befriend it and give it consideration will be those who receive the benefit of its company and experience first-hand the extra edge of its presence.

The wise, then, known when to negotiate and when to compromise. They know the strength or weakness of their position and whether their opponent is all talk or not.

Truth, timing and context are all taken into consideration before the choice is made.

Eisenhower, in order to get his way on the method and timing of the invasion of German-held Europe, compromised on non-essentials. He also bided his time with the constantly chafing General Montgomery.

Yet when victory beckoned and disunity amongst the allies threatened the final stages of the campaign, he refused to budge. He held his ground, knowing that not only was he right but that Roosevelt and Churchill would have to support him. Montgomery finally realised this and thus gave his full support to Eisenhower's leadership. As Adlai Stevenson states, 'A wiseman who stands firm is a statesman. A foolish man who stands firm is a catastrophe.'

Another example of such cunning is found in ancient times in the life of Solom of Athens.

Appointed chief magistrate in the sixth century B.C., he was honest and good, and provided stable government in a time of unrest. He abolished slavery, extended the vote, encouraged trade, regulated the market, established laws for inherited property, civil rights and penalties for crime. Then he was able to get the Athenian council to vow they would uphold his reforms for a period of ten years. Up to this point he had been wise, now he became cunning. He simply took off! He sailed into voluntary exile for a decade under the pretence of travelling to see the world. He could have stayed on, but knew that the petitions and pressure groups to change and modify the laws that had been established would be incessant. To deny them all would cause ill-will. Therefore, knowing they could not be repealed without his signature, he moved on. His life reveals not only an absence of ambition, but the shrewd use of this common sense aspect of the wise in heart.

ENDNOTES

1   Matthew 10:16.
2   Machiavelli, *The Prince* , Penguin 1995, XVIII p 55.

Chapter 11

INTUITION
The Wisdom of Revelation

Intuition is somewhat of a mystery. We all are aware of its existence, but where it comes from and where it goes are questions whose answers remain in the mist. We perceive that it has more to do with perceiving than learning. We discover it as it emerges, from time to time, out of its dwelling place in the subconscious, but then it quickly shrinks from view.

Wisdom is more than cerebral exercise. The heart is involved with its production and application. It makes use of the mind and desperately needs it in the same way a car cannot run on an empty tank. Yet the engine, the generator of wisdom, is found further in and deeper still.

If wisdom was simply a matter of brain cells then successful college graduation would be its necessary prerequisite. Yet, many have knowledge, few have wisdom. The wise are found in all walks of life. Indeed, one could argue their numbers are greater amongst those with no or little formal education.

Wisdom cannot be reduced to chemical formulas or located somewhere in the cerebrum. Like courage or integrity, it is found only within the soul.

Throughout the history of literature, the terms 'wisdom' and 'heart' have always been connected, whereas wisdom and head, whilst related, have little of the same poetry about them. The former are lovers, the latter simply acquaintances. Like the old saying about love and marriage: 'They go together.' So, 'Wiseheart' would have been an appropriate title for this book. 'Wisehead' lacks both euphony and energy. Only the heart can wield aright both the depth and the discernment that is wisdom. The area of intuition is where this truth is clearly seen.

The phrase 'woman's intuition' is well known. Yet whether gender is a major player in the utilisation of intuition remains to be seen. I like what one wit said:

'Intuition: that strange instinct that tells a woman she is right, whether she is or not.'

This particular quote remains anonymous. Its author choosing thus, for obvious reasons!

In the discussion of this attribute of wisdom, several questions come to the fore. Can intuition be trusted? Can it be nurtured and encouraged? And, if so, how? We all understand the relevance of these questions, as there is something magical about the intuitive sense. To suddenly be aware and know... and know not how, sends a special thrill through our beings. It is almost a spiritual experience. We recognise that the flash of insight came from somewhere beyond the cortex and that we disregard it at our peril.

SO, CAN IT BE TRUSTED?

I believe that intuition grows out of the seedbed of the heart. It is the product of our inner world and the child of our deepest musings. Therefore, any questions concerning its trustworthiness have to do with the make-up of the soil or the quality of the spirit. Yet, what do we mean by trustworthy? Are we speaking of truth or morality? For example, one's intuition may tell you that the married woman next door would sleep with you if pursued, or that the bank down the road is best robbed early in the morning. Both of these things may be true, but neither of them are right. Could it be that intuition works in the direction your life is pointing, its character being no better than its possessor. If this is the case, then intuition is merely a servant of the life. Its framework, parameters and moral code are those that it discovers within the life of its holder. Jesus spoke just a little of this concept when he said: 'The good man brings good things out of the good stored up in him and the evil man brings evil things out of the evil stored up in him.'[1]

So it seems to me that intuition is a good guide of what is true but it may not be a good indicator of what is honourable or right. The power of the heart propels the life in the direction that is set. Up or down, positive or negative. Our values, beliefs, intellectual and spiritual nourishment therefore are not trivial matters. Whatever the life is intent on, intuition will work towards. It has been designed for great good, but like anything to do with humanity it is easily tainted with sin or selfishness. Isaiah Berlin, the Russian-born English philosopher, wrote an essay entitled, 'The Crooked Timber of Humanity.'[2] He makes the point that no straight thing can come from twisted wood. Therefore, our fantasies of Utopia are just that, fantasies. The perfect omelette can never be made, for all the eggs carry within them subtle flaws. Our hearts have cracks in them and inner wholesomeness is more an ideal than a reality.

Is there no hope then for conscience or intuition? Are we doomed to forever muddle through the mire? I believe that growth, wholeness, health and cleansing are available to us all. Yet this requires our longing for such, and a willingness to call out for help, in sincerity and faith, to the only one I know who has the answers for the human soul. Call it prayer, or call it spirituality, but it seems answers to questions like these only come from above.

INTUITION IN THE MARKET PLACE

Increasingly in our time, intuition has played a major role in successful decision-making. The technology-propelled flood of information has made it simply impossible to know all relevant facts prior to choice. Add to this the accelerating pace of change and one begins to understand why wise leaders and successful managers have leant more and more on intuitive reasoning. John Sculley, when asked about his decision-making processes at Apple Computer, said: 'It's very intuitive. Just like a sailor can sniff the air and knows when a storm is coming up, I have always been good at sniffing the air and knowing when the time is right to change a course direction or when to make a big investment.'

Lee Iacocca, another well known decisive leader would agree:

'You never get all the facts. If you wait, by the time you do get them, your facts will be out of date because the market has moved on... At some time, you have to take the leap of faith... because even the right decision is wrong if its made too late.'

This is recognised more and more within the business world. Personality tests and business books now feature whole sections on intuition. Several volumes have been written recently whose only subject was that of the power of intuition. Ron Schultz's 'Unconventional Wisdom,' the study of twelve innovators, explaining how intuition has revolutionised their decision-making, is a good case in point.[3] Talk to any great leader worth his or her salt about this very fact and you will find that after the analysis and the debate, after the talking and the savvy presentations, the key decisions are always made from the gut.

DEVELOPING INTUITION

Louis Pasteur once said, 'Fortune favours the prepared mind making it ripe for discovery.' It seems one can get ready for the flash of insight. Yet when or how it will come, we know not. An idea in the middle of the night, a mental image whilst out for a walk, a funny thought as you look into a shop window. Yet when it arrives one must grab it, take it and use it for it may not come your way again. This can be annoying at times, for inspiration can call at inconvenient moments. Why is it that a sudden idea for a new chapter comes often to me just as I am going to sleep. I know I will not remember it in the morning, so up I get, grab my pen, and write while I can. Yet when I am ready to write with a day stretching before me the blank page seems to laugh in my face. Martha Graham, the late world-renowned choreographer has said:

'There's no such thing as the bulb suddenly going on, you must prepare your mind for intuition.'

The mood of both Pasteur's and Graham's statements are very much toward the cultivation of this aspect of wisdom.

There are things that we can do that will enhance intuition in our lives. Primary among them would be the habit of listening. So often the whispers from within are lost in the chatter of our own cyberspace. The neck-top computer is constantly on the go and incoming email from the heart often finds the line engaged. The wise of heart, therefore, give time to contemplation, to walks in the wood and to quiet evenings with the television off. I think this is the key practice in developing an intuitive edge. Others have written books on various exercises for intuitive growth. Yet for me this journey of discovery and learning is highly subjective. Brainstorming or book reading, solitude or sharing, all of us need to find what unlocks the door of our own heart. We can, however, be confident in the knowledge that there is more to us than meets the eye. Logic and reason are not the only weapons in our arsenal. As Schopenhauer once said,

'There is in us something wiser than our heads.'[4]

ENDNOTES

1   Matthew 12:35.
2   Isaiah Berlin, *The Crooked Timber of Humanity*, John Murray, London, 1990.
3   Don Schultz, *Unconventional Wisdom*, Harper & Collins, 1994.
4   Schopenhauer, *Councils and Maxims Parerga and Paralipomena*, 1851.

THE APPLICATION
OF WISDOM

Chapter 12
SEX

Freud thought the power of sexuality was the strongest force we have to deal with in life. Many would disagree, but all can understand how someone could come to that conclusion.

Novelist Frederick Buechner referred to it as:

'An ape that gibbers in my loins.'

We cannot ignore it or dispose of it. It resists training and the more we attend to it, the more unruly it becomes. Buechner continues:

'Tame him as we will by day, he rages all the wilder in our dreams at night. Just when we think we're safe from him, he raises up his ugly head and smirks, and there's no river in the world flows cold and strong enough to strike him down. Almighty God, why dost thou deck men out with such a loathsome toy?'[1]

Pure sex energy is a wild horse, a raging river, a runaway train. The metaphor may be varied but the meaning is the same. The power of sex can dismantle our life faster and with more fury than almost anything else. When it is unleashed it seems that normal, rational human beings will sacrifice anything to its insistence. The judge who sabotages a career, marriage and a lifetime's reputation for a few moments of illicit pleasure in some public toilet; the spouse who strays and becomes addicted to a secretive and soul-destroying double life; the minister caught in a web of pornography; the tragic life of the outer facade of respectability camouflaging the inner world of lonely lust.

Yet, the human being is not an animal, subject only to hormones and mating patterns. Love, purpose and discipline will uncover new dimensions within us. Those who are spiritually inclined would say that we possess a soul, that inherently by God's design there is more to us than meets the eye. In the same way that living, breathing creatures are different from plants, so we are different from the animal world. We are more than just another species.

Human history declares this truth to be self-evident. We can control our bodies and thwart our feelings if the need or want is with us. 'If it feels good do it' is no way to live, as the drug addict, alcoholic or spouse beater will testify.

IT'S GOT EVERYBODY'S ATTENTION

Let's face it, sex has too much air time. It rates, sells and titillates well, creating its own market with addictive power. Programmers and news editors give it top billing. It peeks at us from the lingerie catalogues and the fashion magazines. From the health club to the hotel, from the jokes of the D.J. to the walls of public toilets, everything seems suggestive and many sections of the media have become, as a result, monothematic. The pendulum has swung too far. The repression, fear and sexism that ruled in the 40s needed to be changed. Maybe the sexual revolution was the revolution we had to have. As Lewis Lapham writes:

'In 1947 genetics was a subject that had to do with mice, a woman's place was in the home and sex was something that happened in France.'[2]

Yet something has gone terribly wrong with this march towards freedom. The young buy the ads and live out their tragic consequences. I well remember the news story recently of an eighteen-year-old who had a child during her graduation dance. In a break in the music she gave birth to the baby in the bathroom, put it in the waste basket, washed her hands and returned for the next number. Lapham suggests that the girl's actions are the logical conclusion of our consumer market: 'Sex is merchandising and the product of desire and, like Kleenex, is disposable. In the garden of tabloid delights, there is always a clean towel and another song... The market can't tell the difference between adultery and a programme of aerobic exercise. It doesn't know or care who said what to whom, or whether the whip was meant to be used on a horse from Kentucky or a gentleman from Toledo.'[3]

The market, you see, is amoral and its perspective has become society's view at large. For anyone to speak out on moral grounds is seen as narrow, prejudicial or repressive. Sex is not, however, as harmless as fitness machines or facial cream. Yet it is sold and promoted with no warning attached. Smoking can cause cancer, but sex can destroy multiple lives. It promises ecstasy, but its pathway is fraught with peril. It is more than anatomy or biology. Dissecting frogs is generally not addictive and does not result in disease or unwanted pregnancy. Yet we group it all together and proclaim information without morality, passion without borders, pleasure without control. Lapham again writes:

'About the perils of the voyage to paradise, the old moral guide books were not wrong. What at first glance looks like a ticket to the islands of bliss often proves more nearly to resemble a reserved seat in one of the eight dress circles of Dante's inferno. I think of the numbers of people I have known over the last twenty or thirty years who sacrificed themselves on the altars of the imaginary self: marooned in a desolate marriage, so paralysed by so many sexual options, that nothing ever came of their talent and ambition, dead of AIDS at the age of thirty-one.'[4]

Sex has this kind of power. All of us are susceptible to its urges. To presume immunity is to walk headlong into its jaws. Proverbs speaks of its power with the warning:

'Many are the victims she has brought down, many mighty are among her slain.'[5]

The point is, we do not and we cannot resist the flood unless we cling to wisdom and draw our strength from one another and from above. Like a yacht with no keel is a life with no heart-felt values. The winds of greed and lust will blow us onto the reefs every time. The wise heart still leans in the strengthening breeze, but is impelled forward not sideways. Wisdom means living by conviction not preference, by values and beliefs not feelings or fancies.

The fire of passion should not, and cannot, be extinguished but it must be controlled and sexuality channelled. When our sex drive rules us it does so with evil intention, imprisoning rather than enriching our lives. One of the greatest lies ever told is that of the supposed utopia of the totally liberated, morally free sex-life.

The hard evidence of such a life is that it is one where pleasure is diminishing and true joy is forgotten. One recovering sex addict put it this way: 'I quickly learned that lust... points in only one direction. You cannot go back to a lower level and stay satisfied. Always you want more... I've experienced enough of the unquenchable nature of sex to frighten me for good. Lust does not satisfy; it stirs up. I no longer wonder how deviants can get into child molesting, masochism and other abnormalities. Although such acts are incomprehensible to me, I remember well where I ended up was also incomprehensible to me when I started.

'A cousin of mine subscribes to at least fifteen of the raunchiest magazines I have ever seen... He has told me that, even surrounded by vivid depictions of every sex act, every size and shape of woman he can imagine, he still wants more. He still devours the new issues. He and his wife are experimenting with orgies now, and numerous other variations I won't mention. It is not enough. The thrill will fade before long, and he will want more.'[6]

Like drinking salt water to satisfy thirst, those who allow the wild animal to rule are constantly discontented and disempowered. True pleasure and real sex are found not in the dark alleys and the seedy night spots. Under the flashing of those neon lights there is no real laughter.

There is a huge difference between making love and just having sex. Steve Biddulph in his book, Manhood, put it this way:

'There are, it seems, orgasms and orgasms.'[7]

In the same way that we are more than animals so sex is more than physical. Our schools tend to teach the subject as if it was simply a subdivision of biology or chemistry. Sex is not, however, as a starkly minimalist definition suggests: 'A penis and a vagina going out on a date.' When we make love to someone we are becoming one with that person. We are giving of ourselves and imparting of our very souls. As one man lamented after a decade of casual liaisons: 'I feel I have left little bits of myself all over the place.'

John Smith, writer, thinker and president of the Christian bikie gang, The God Squad, tells of one conversation he had with a girl after he had spoken on the power of sex to a teenage audience. She explained that they had recently been on an overnight school outing into the city: 'We were taken to see a show and there was a lot of nudity in it and afterwards a bunch of us ended up together in a room where things got out of hand and now... now I feel dirty. Is that all sex is? Is it like when dogs do it on the grass?'

I am not sure why or how it happens but what we do with our bodies affects our hearts. It matters not if logically and rationally we have dealt with the morality of it at all, or if we have even considered if sex was anything other than simply two bodies connecting. We don't break this law, it breaks us. We have, over the years, tried to escape its implications. We have tried to be free and tolerant, we have even worked toward making sexual promiscuity within marriage the 'in' thing to believe. Yet these efforts all fail in the long run and we are forced to return to the guiding principles of love, commitment and monogamy.

One newspaper columnist sounded the alarm several years ago. At the time it seemed, all talk of morals were patronisingly put down as being the echoes of a darker, less urbane age. A new book redefining marriage was the topic of his comments, and his words merit deep consideration:

'Open Marriage', by George and Nena O'Neill, was a book for the times and it said over and over again that you should be honest, straight, out-front, give space, let the other person do their thing, communicate, and if you wanted to have an affair, for God's sake, do be honest about it: don't sneak around, make excuses, call late in the afternoon with some cock-and-bull story about work. Simply pick up the phone and say, 'Honey, I'll be a bit late tonight. I'm going to have an affair.

'But there were these couples I know. They were open. They were honest. They were having affairs. They were not sneaking around (applause), they were not lying (applause), they were being honest (whistles). They were being open. Everyone agreed that it was wonderful. The men agreed and the women agreed and I agreed and it all made you wonder. Then they split. There was something wrong. Invariably, someone couldn't take it. It has nothing to do with the head. The head understood. It was the heart; it was, you should pardon the expression, broken.

'It all makes you think. It makes you think that maybe there are things we still don't know about men and women and maybe before we spit in the eye of tradition we ought to know what we're doing. I have some theories and one of them is that one of the ways you measure love is not with words, but with actions, with commitment, with what you are willing to give up, with what you are willing to share with no one else.'[8]

The lust-filled life is a life which is slowly seeping away. Gradually perspectives and feelings are changed so that the cheap thrill of the centrefold or the girl at the strip club become the only thing that thrills us. Yet, decreasingly so, for the slave of libido finds their master has taken over every part of their lives.

I read recently the journey of one man who wrote candidly of his own realisation that his life had been devoured by this particular demon. He had just finished a business engagement in Boston and was to spend the next three days driving up the coast of Maine. On his last night in the city he visited a peep show where for twenty-five cents one can view, from an enclosed booth, a naked woman on a revolving platform.

'Maybe such booths do serve a redeeming purpose for society: by exposing lust in its basic demythologised form. There is no art or beauty, no acrobatic dancing. The woman is obviously a sex object and nothing else. The men are isolated, caged voyeurs. There is no relationship, no teasing... and yet, there I was, a respected member of society, dropping in quarters like a frantic, long-distance caller at a pay phone.

'What shocked me more was my trip up the coast. I followed my usual practice of staying in homey inns with big fireplaces, and of eating by the waterfront and watching the sailboats bob in the shimmering sea, of taking long solitary walks on the rocky promontories where huge waves crashed with thunder, of closing my eyes and letting salt splash across my face, of stopping at roadside stands for fresh lobster and crab. There was a difference this time: I felt no pleasure. None. My emotional reaction was the same as if I had been at home, yawning, reading the newspaper. The reaction disturbed me profoundly. By all counts, those wonderful, sensuous experiences rated far higher than the cheap thrill of watching an overweight, pock-marred body rotate on plywood. And yet, to my utter disbelief, my mind kept roaming back to that grimy booth in Boston. Was I going crazy? Would I lose every worthwhile sensation in life? Was my soul leaking away? Was I becoming possessed?'[9]

It is amazing to me how this happens, but happen it does. How do the grimy, smut-filled images imprint themselves more than majestic mountains or picturesque seascapes? We trade gold for mud, and this loss of perspective can only be the result of inner blindness, for the clear-eyed laugh at such wrong choice. We must wake up and realise that life is more than accumulation or pleasure seeking. Dreams, destiny, eternity will be left on the shelf if we spend the energy and force of our souls on such petty pursuits.

The road to destiny stretches before us. It is clear and firm, yet it regularly leads over the horizon and we see neither its end or the joy along its path. Thus we are easy prey to the fatal distraction of inappropriate yet magnetic out-of-line sexuality. We prefer, if you like, to play in the muddy verges on the side of the road, to splash in the puddles and make grimy little castles and think that maybe by so doing we are enjoying life. All we have done is detoured. Our highway to destiny remains by our side and until we get out of the ditch and move forward along its daunting pathway we will never experience that which we were designed for.

So, how does the pursuer of wisdom navigate the troubled and powerful waters of libido? The following principles are those that we should hold in our consciousness if we desire to both cherish and channel our sexuality.

1. Don't Underestimate Sexuality's Power

The curious often become the captive. The surge of sex-energy will swamp the unsuspecting soul. The trick here is not to see how close one can get to promiscuity without crossing the line. Flirting has its own fascination but, like a whirlpool, the longer you play at its edge the more you are caught in its current. I remember the story of the hiring process for the Pony Express across the Rockies. In those pre-railroad days the sole connection between east and west was the horse and carriage. The roads were treacherous and the mountain passes required the greatest skill from the horsemen and women. The job, due to the hard times, attracted many applicants. One young man, after spending several hours in the queue and finally reaching the hiring manager, was highly pessimistic: 'I don't think it's even worth talking to me. I am obviously not the best driver.' 'Why do you say that?' the older gentleman replied. 'Well, the talk in the queue was rather intimidating,' he responded. 'They were all talking about how close to the edge they can guide the stagecoach when riding the high passes... My philosophy has always been to see how far away from it I can get.' There was a short pause, then the manager smiled and simply said, 'You're hired!'

Such is the case with sexuality. How far one can get away from danger, from adultery, from lingering eyes and second glances, is the key to success in this arena. The tiger is fierce, strong, and pounces suddenly. To run is smart. To treat its threat with casual aloofness is stupid to the extreme.

2. Control the Imagination

The world of thought is a wonderful world. Better than Disneyland and more powerful than the latest digital movie. Our imagination can transport us around the world and plant images that will bring both fear or fun into our lives. Sex is never merely a physical thing. It starts with a thought. The slow mental undressing of the beauty, and the longing for intimate involvement. Yet such images can get away from us. One cannot start knocking over dominos and then just stop the sequence as it nears the danger zone. It is a lot safer and easier to recognise domino one and give it a wide berth.

Wisdom recognises that mental whispers lead to thoughts, which lead to fantasy, which in turn will begin to find physical actualisation in some way. The pornographic film and magazine industry is fuelled by the thoughts of lonely and fractured people throughout the world. It feeds off their hurt and need and, in turn, adds more fuel to their fire. Year by year the cycle increases strength and the sheer volume of material reveals both the degree of the problem and the extent of its pervasiveness. The statistics are alarming. In 1996, for instance, in America alone, 7,852 new pornographic movies were released. (This compares with the 471 general releases out of Hollywood.)

The answer, then, to this invasion and the general availability of such material is to guard our thoughts, for it is thought that feeds the frenzy. I only notice chocolate and the latest Cadbury's ad when I am thinking and drooling over 'le chocolat' or am at least open to its suggestion. When I am not, they blend into the background. Attention gives rise to action and not the other way around.

3. Intentionalise in the Other Direction

Controlling one's mind is not so much about not thinking on something, but focusing the mind and imagination on something else. The New Testament speaks about concentrating mental energy in a positive direction: 'Whatever is true, whatever is noble, whatever is right, whatever is pure... think about such things.'[10]

I don't know if you have ever tried not to think about something, but it proves to be deceptively difficult. For example, think about a large blue elephant, picture it walking through the jungle or smoking a cigar as it lounges on an easy chair. Got the image? Now start to not think about the elephant. See its cigar go out and its image evaporate. Remove the elephant from the screen of your mind... The more one tries to not see, the more the image returns. Now picture a white unicorn racing through the streets of New York, crowds gathering, helicopters hovering, children smiling... What happened to the elephant? The moral of the story is not that the unicorns of Manhattan are more powerful than nicotine-affected elephants, only that the present thought will always dominate the previous.

The way to not think on the one thing is to think on the other. The way to not think on the evil is to think on the good. The way to remove worry and pessimism is simply to actively and intentionally think optimistically and hopefully. We cannot consider a certain body as the subject of our lust whilst at the same time meditating on the fact that they are a person, that they have thoughts and dreams, hurts and joys. Research has shown that the only way to help the sexually obsessive or those who fantasise with paedophilia and the like, is to alter their thinking processes. The wise hearted thus cultivate wholesome thinking habits and choose to meditate on that which will bring health not hurt, on that which will fuel destiny rather than feed lust, on that which will take us to where we want to go and not derail us into the despair and oblivion of an out-of-control sexuality.

4. Develop A Healthy Heart

The reason many are susceptible to the whims and whispers of hormones is that something is broken on the inside. Dysfunctional families, fear of fathers, or a longing for affection create voids in one's life that the allure of lust promises to fill. We sense our hurt and our need and, rather than looking for solutions that go to the source of the problem, we choose the anaesthesia of orgasm or casual romance.

This is why the support group, the counsellor and the church are so successful in curbing the lust-driven life. They try to get at the cause, rather than just treat the symptoms. Lack of love, dashed hopes, loss of warmth and spiritual void will all manifest themselves in our lives and our sexuality will frequently take the brunt of such loneliness or discontent.

Wisdom simply recognises that a problem in the area of sexuality may not be a problem in the area of sexuality. Heart issues are the foundation of successful living. Control over the force of body urges comes from within rather than from without.

5. Be Willing To Get Help

There is great shame attached to this very personal area of our lives. Yet wisdom would demand that we regain control. If that means getting external help, then the sooner the better. The repercussions of a sexually out-of-balance life are immense. Getting healthy should not be a low priority.

When our car has problems we go to the mechanic. If our photocopier or computer starts fouling up we do not hesitate to call in the experts. Yet when that which really matters needs attention, be it a marriage, relationship or self-diminishing habit, we run for cover. Secrecy, and the reluctance to enlist the support of professionals, friends or God, will do nothing in moving us towards freedom. All it will accomplish is more shame, more compulsion and more pain.

I have discovered one of the keys to health, whatever kind we are talking about, is learning and objectivity. We must read the books, talk to those who have proficiency, and be willing to be both vulnerable and accountable. The mirey world of permissive or deviant sexuality can only be escaped from with the helping hand of someone else. They must be above us or beside us, and have their feet on solid ground. Placing our faith in God and others, and following their consequent encouragements and directions, will cause us slowly but surely to discover a whole new dimension of life. A life where our sex drives are celebrated, not cowered from. Where we become our true selves and that which has pressed us and controlled us is finally put into its rightful place.

ENDNOTES

1   Frederick Buechner, *Godric, Chatto & Windus*, London, 1981, p 153.

2   Lewis Lapham, *The Garden of Tabloid Delights*, Harpers, August 1997.

3   Ibid, Harpers.

4   Ibid, Harpers.

5   Proverbs 7:26.

6   Anonymous, 'The War Within', *Leadership Journal*, Fall 1982, Vol. 3 No. 4, p 30.

7   Steve Biddulph, *Manhood*, Finch Publishing, Sydney, 1994, p 49.

8   Richard Cohen, 'Open Marriage... Broken Marriage', *The Washington Post*, 1977, as quoted by Charles Swindoll, *Strike the Original Match*, Living Books, Wheaton, illinois, 1989, p 46.

9   Ibid, *The War Within*.

10 1 Philippians 4:8.

Chapter 13

HABITS

'We are what we repeatedly do; excellence, then, is not an act but a habit.'
Aristotle

Bad habits haunt us, good habits enrich us. The trouble and the wonder of habit is that they do so every day. We can all get over the one-off event, the 'annus horribilis', but bad habits are here to stay. The great events like marriage ceremonies or the birth of children sparkle in our consciousness for a time, but then slowly fade. The memories of the good and the scars of the bad remain with us to our dying day, yet they do not go on living with us in the same way habits do. Habits grow strand by strand, hour by hour, and can either be powerful cords that pull us forward or terrible fetters that bind and entangle us. Wisdom is about building the habits that will enhance our lives and destroying those that would bring paralysis.

Progress towards success or destruction has always been a step at a time. Instant riches or overnight achievement are mainly myths. No, it is the constant plodding, the continual yet slow movement, inch by inch, day by day, that finally will accomplish the task. Turtles win by habit, hares by impulse. Yet impulses come infrequently whereas habits can be cultivated and will perform week-in and week-out. As my Greek teacher used to say: 'It's the daily dose that does it.'

Small steps toward the goal are better than none at all. My grandmother is a good case in point. About three years ago she started walking a mile a day and now, over a thousand days later... we haven't got the foggiest idea where she is! This regularity of action coupled with the passing of time equals greatness. On the other hand, genius and favourable circumstance can always be waiting, full of promise, but never performing.

Thus the power of habit, for good or evil, cannot be underestimated. By it great books have been written and famous crimes have been committed. It is responsible for the tobacco industry and the fitness phenomena. With its aid many track to skid row whilst others ride its power into spiritual growth or financial independence. Habits are both the unseen champions and the unrealized culprits of modern society.

One of the objections raised to the habit-governed life is that of the perceived loss of spontaneity and sparkle. The habitual individual who rises at the same time each day, travels to work the same way and sits at the same Dilbert-style cubicle year-in, year-out, is the stuff of nightmare. Woe unto us if this attribute of wisdom was all about a pedantic, monotonous, 'life in a rut' experience. I, for one, would be heading to the party of the fools where I would at least see some variety and enjoy again the thrill of surprise.

There are the many varieties of personality tests on the market today that categorise people based on where they place themselves on various continuums. One of these illustrates the difference between the structured and unstructured, the organised and disorganised.

The structured soul finds peace more accessible when the appointment calender is bedded down three months out, the holiday accommodation six months ahead, and the airport reached at least two hours before the flight. The unstructured, on the other hand, are never happier than when the calender has multiple options, the holiday is on a 'take each day or country as it comes' attitude, and the airport is reached just in the nick of time. I am proud to number myself among this latter and happy throng. I delight in new places, journeying on new roads and avoiding routine living. I have even had several restaurants refuse my credit card on account of the signature varying. Yet the unstructured should not be the haphazard. In the same way, the structured should not be the predictable.

The habit-based life is not one which lacks pizazz or panache, it is simply a life that works out what are the important things that one must do; saving, thinking, giving... and then does them in exciting and everchanging ways. The widom then, gives attention to the developing of life-growing habits and is always on the lookout to curb the embryonic, yet potentially fatal, darker ones.

ENLISTING THE POSITIVES

The power of positive habit is remarkable. Yet the wonder of good habits is given little air time. Certainly not as much as the fight against their negative twin. The books and, for that matter, the songs tend to be about 'bad' habits. Support groups and entire organisations are given over to the destruction of the negative ones yet scarcely a word is said regarding the cultivation of the positive. I first began to realise the primacy of this task when I read of Benjamin Franklin's thirteen weeks. He realised that to reach the destination he felt was intended for him, he had to give attention to his heart and character. Thus, he devised a systematic programme which operated in his life for many decades and was, in his own words, 'the chief cause of all my accomplishments.' He chose what he believed to be thirteen ingredients of good character... courage, humility, patience, discipline and the like. He then gave a week to the conscious cultivation of each virtue. His reading, thinking and self-analysis was focused on each ingredient week by week in turn. Every thirteen weeks the cycle began again. Thus, four weeks a year were given in concentration to each foundation for successful living. Is it any wonder that he soared as he did? How many others would do the same if they simply gave attention to such matters? Wisdom recognises this truth and acts upon it. The methods may be different but the end remains the same: inner growth and a healthy heart.

RESISTING THE NEGATIVE

The force of imprinted habit is a force not easily confronted or defeated. Neural pathways of frequent action will quickly turn trends into tollways; they become both mandatory and expensive. Those suffering with any sort of addictive behaviour understand this point well. Habits resist their breaking. New roads are hard to build, and again and again the psyche returns to the course which is both familiar and damaging. So how do the wise go about the destruction of unwanted habit? It is a question worth considering as many have tried with great passion and longing, yet still fail to grasp their freedom.

I remember spending an evening talking with a good friend of mine on this very subject. A friend who had considerable experience both in his own personal journey, and also helping thousands around the world break free from addictive and soul-destroying activities. Sy Rogers had lived as a woman for several years. Scheduled for a sex-change operation, he lived an androgynous life embroiled in that dark and hazy world of gender confusion and gay promiscuity. His remarkable story is one of dramatic internal revolution that caused the projectory of his life to swing

180 degrees. He has moved from confusion to clarity, from homosexuality to heterosexuality, from multiple lonely liaisons to a happy marriage. His time is now divided between a burgeoning music career and speaking to those who are sexually broken and desiring change. His approach is both refreshing and effective. Although a committed Christian, he never riles against the gay, lesbian or transsexual scenes. He simply provides help for those within their number who want to change their life. The results have been amazing and put pay to the lie that however we are, we must remain. It is true that certain behaviours, habits, and neural processes require extraordinary effort and courage to reorientate, but Sy and many others like him are testimony to the fact that the heart can rule the hormones and that grace, God and grit can trump genetics, guilt and generalisation. That night we listed the key aspects that seemed to be necessary in any form of permanent life change. Their application may be varied, but the following principles seems mandatory in all cases.

1. Admit the Need

The first step in moving away from a bad habit or addictive behaviour is to realise you have a problem. The person who declares, 'I am out of control in this area, I need help,' has begun the journey to freedom. This is why the phrase, 'I am an alcoholic,' is a prerequisite to overcoming alcoholism. Indeed, as we have already discovered, the key to getting anything in life is first of all to realise that you don't presently have it. Thus, the fool is one who doesn't recognise his condition. Josh Billings put it this way:

'It ain't what a man don't know that makes him a fool or what he does know, but what he does know that ain't so.'[1]

Until we recognise the need, we will not look for the answer. A casual acknowledgement that there might be a problem will only mean a casual enquiry as to a possible solution. Such a plan is doomed, for to escape the surging currents of ingrained habit requires both the desperate scream for help and a violent lunge towards the shore. Jesus talked about the blessing of God's Kingdom being only available to those who were, 'Poor in spirit.' That is, those who recognise their need for God . Pride here has no place, for its desire to hold both ends of the rescue rope thwarts its deliverance. We are, as Billy Joel said, 'Only human.' Our refusal to admit this does not change the truth. It only means that we close all the doors and make our prison cell more secure.

2. Build Hope

Hope paints a picture of a preferable future. Such an image gives us both a sense of direction and tenacity to continue the journey. Without vision, without seeing things as they could be, one is doomed to live in a never-changing present. This is why stories like Sy's are so empowering for those who struggle with the same kinds of problems. If someone else has forged the way, if another has battled and won, then maybe my struggle will not be in vain. Thus, a new confidence is born, and a determination is shaped. The reading of biography, the listening to others' stories, all add to our resolve, for they paint our potential future with bold and beckoning brush strokes. We must finish the image ourselves and adopt it as our own. Their hope must become 'my hope', but when this picture is finished it also becomes compelling and slowly, almost magnetically, we are drawn forward towards its fulfiling.

3. Desire to Change

In all those who have successfully vanquished their enemies of habit, there has been not only a clear hope but also a strong desire to break free from the past and move towards the new future. I'm not talking of some kind of superficial desire fanned by a stirring sermon or hyped momentarily by the suicide of a friend. This desire must be keen, heart-felt and sustained. Change of great magnitude only occurs when there is a longing almost to the point of obses- sion. Half-heartedness won't get you half-way there, it will get you nowhere. Only the fully devoted, utter- ly convinced, radically committed make it to the final hurdle. If it was easy everyone would be doing it. If it was simple, the power of negative habit would only be illusion. Yet many have conquered and many more will. Only those who are swept along by a desire fanned to fervency can make the decisions. Only the desperate are able to swallow their pride and move forward on the journey. Breaking out of orbit requires extra thrust, so nothing but turbo-powered longing will move us beyond the gravity of a self-diminishing lifestyle.

4. Decision Time

This key is a corollary to the previous one. In fact, the two are intertwined. Desire must be cultivated and decisions must be made. Desire is a constant and journeys with us along the road. Decision is a line we cross and once we have crossed it our resolve is to move on, never to go back. A lackadaisical decision will not do, it must be one of quality. Convenient back doors or escape hatches are welded shut, excuses to fail must be eradicated. It all sounds kind of epic, doesn't it? This talk of destiny, decision and desire, yet all great things happen this way, whether we are climbing mountains, attempting to win a sports tournament or building a successful marriage or family. The worst decision is often no decision.

When life calls the shots and we simply respond, the effort is less, but we will never get to where we want to go. Bertrand Russell put it this way: 'Nothing is so exhausting as indecision and nothing is so futile.'[2]

5. Get Help

Once we are committed, the next stage is to get help, to utilise every valuable resource be it theological, relational or educational. We cannot operate as a closed system. We must be willing to call out to either God above or friends beside, when times of need are upon us. Certainly we must do so, if we are to escape the passions and powers of unwanted behaviour. The mentor, the support group, the close friend, all will add their energy to the cause. There is a need, you see, to bare the soul. Accountability destroys secrecy, reduces pride and reinforces humility... all of which are necessary virtues if permanent change is to become a reality. I have seen many try to set themselves free whilst keeping their struggles totally private. Although we don't have to live in a glass bowl, there must be some who know, who understand and who care. The secretive road leads to a dead end. 'We are unable, it seems, to pick ourselves up,' in the words of Ravi Zacharias, 'by our own metaphysical bootstraps.' I'm not sure why this is the case. Maybe it is because the subjective view is always distorted or, perhaps, that only through synergy there is enough power to propel us forward. It may have something to do with how we are designed. We are made for community and only find ourselves in the reflection of those around us.

John Donne's celebrated poem still has great lessons to teach us in this individualistic age.

> 'No man is an island, entire of itself;
> every man is a piece of the continent,
> a part of the main,
> if a clod be washed away by the sea,
> Europe is the less...
> Any man's death diminishes me,
> because I am involved in mankind;

and therefore never send to know
for whom the bell tolls, it tolls for thee.'[3]

So the call needs to be made, the counsellor contacted or the group attended. Those who go it alone will only move backwards and their hopes slowly turn from positive expectation to cruel fantasy.

6. Educate Yourself

This point is almost a subcategory of the previous one, but it seems to be the case that the more information we can gain about the issues we are dealing with, the more light is shed on our pathway. Learning about causes, personality types, family of origin difficulties and the struggle of others all seem to firm our resolve, make broader our way and fine tune our strategy. Now, it is important to realise that knowledge alone will not cause change, for reason by itself cannot curb behaviour. This is step six in a seven-step process. Its a little bit like adding a spoiler to the back of a racing car. It simply enhances the speed and helps in the cornering and manoeuvrability. It is taken for granted the car already has an engine and a driver.

7. Persevere

Sy's journey took seven years. Some travel longer, others shorter, but all have to persevere. This is not about instant change. The trouble with gradualism is that it is so... well, gradual. One can begin to think

170

that nothing much is happening. The book is written a letter at a time, the mountain climbed a step at a time, the web is spun a strand at a time and a life is forged a day at a time. This long continuance in the same direction will eventually take us into the promised land. Detours abound, unexpected road-blocks appear, but the persistent soul continues on, clambering over, tunnelling through. No thought is given to U-turns or side-of-the-road picnic spots. Onward and upward is the call.

Although Thomas Edison is applying the following comments on persistence to action and creativity, they are also instructive within our present context.

'When a man makes up his mind to solve any problem, he may at first meet opposition; but if he holds on and keeps on searching, he will be sure to find some sort of solution. The trouble with most people is that they quit before they start. In all my experiences, I do not recall having ever found the solution to any problem connected with my work on my first attempt. And one of the most surprising things is the fact that when I have discovered the thing for which I am searching, I generally find that it has been within my reach all the time; but nothing except persistence and a will to win would have revealed it.'

Now, again, we must remember that persistence is part of the package, not the whole thing. It is persistence in doing the right thing that will make the difference. To persevere in the wrong direction simply means that you move further away from your objective. So, persistence divorced from direction simply compounds the problem. Just continuing to do is of no merit, for fools continue with foolishness and, on their journey, will discover no headwind. No, the idea of persistence contains within it that of 'battling against', overcoming opposing forces and moving into new territory. Once we have determined that this new territory is on the way to our destination then push on we must. For who knows, another mile, another day, another horizon, when suddenly we will see the lights of home twinkling in the twilight.

ENDNOTES

1   Josh Billings, *Complete Work of Josh Billings*, G.W.
    Dillingham, New York, 1888.
2   Bertrand Russell, *The Conquest of Happiness*, Allen &
    Unwin, London, 1961.
3   John Donne, *Devotions upon Emergent Occasions*, McGill-
    Queen's University Press, 1975, Meditation 17.

Chapter 14

TIME

Jean Paul Satre spoke of two different kinds of time: that which we measure with clocks and watches; and that which we actually live.

Wisdom differentiates between the two and is careful not to allow the former to dictate to the latter. The Greek language, as well, has two words to describe the phenomena of time, one for the moment (kairos), the other for the ticking of the clock (chronos).

Our world, it seems is dominated by the analysis of time rather than time itself. We are continually pressed by the supposed lack of time. We talk of being in a rat race, on a treadmill, and living during rush hour. We have fast food, instant potatoes and overnight delivery. One comic remarked how a friend of his put instant coffee into a microwave and had a time reversal! Yet, the more time we save, the less we seem to have. We are harried and hurried, frantic and frenetic, irritable and agitated. In Tennyson's great poem, 'Ulysses', he talks of 'living life to the lees'. For many of us, however, we don't even get time to uncork the bottle!

Wisdom would encourage us to develop a fresh perspective of time. A philosophy of life which is not dominated by beeping and buttons, or mesmerised by the constant falling of sands through the hour-glass.

JUXTAPOSITION

We live in the present yet our world is neither new nor old but a vivid combination of the two. The hymnals were the first to draw our attention to this with their range of songs, both 'ancient and modern'. Yet today, our whole life moves back and forth between these two variables.

I am writing on Eurostar, the superfast train that travels between London and Paris in just three hours. The field we just whizzed by at 300kmph contained a lone French farmer, working furrow by furrow with a single-blade, horse-drawn plough. Intent on his work and no doubt enjoying his day as much as ours, he was oblivious to us, the new millennium sweeping by. On the train we have speed and comfort. Yet a hasty look around our carriage shows we also have multiple problems. The couple across the way are freezing one another out while their children argue over the latest electronic game. The overweight businessman on his third coffee of the morning looks a little frazzled as he feverishly works the laptop. On

board there is loneliness and lust, ulcers and ennui...
Now, I am not saying the farmer's life is devoid of
angst. Yet the pace and simplicity of his life seem
healthier to me. The jug of wine and the fresh
baguette on his table will probably prove more
hearty and enjoyable than the meals being eaten in
the fine restaurants of Mayfair or Madelaine.

The modern and postmodern ages do not produce
happiness and fulfilment. More often than not they
conjure up pictures of busyness and rush. This era of
progress can be a mirage. Our faith in it can easily
disappoint. We have extra speed and convenience to
get through the day yet we have not stopped to experience our life. Call me a Luddite if you wish, but I
think I would actually enjoy the old world more.

The farmer in the field may well live longer and
revel in life better, yet I will never know. For I am a
child of a mixed marriage, having a desire for the former, but addicted to the latter. I need my gadgets,
conveniences and comforts: from cappuccino to central locking.

The line separating new and old runs through my
heart and thus I blend all things, hoping to have the
best of both. Old-fashioned service on the 747.
Traditional steak and kidney pie in the centrally heat-
ed pub. Natural farm fresh vegetables, as close as the
local 24-hour supermarket.

There are those, however, who extol the virtues of
the past over the present, or vice versa. Not content
to straddle the fence or live with such intriguing contradiction, they try to stay in one zone and demonise
the other.

The progressives remind us that the old days contained bubonic plague, child slavery and shallow sewerage. The conservatives, on the other hand, point to AIDS, inner-city ghettos and the Greenhouse Effect to make their point. They are, of course, both right. Technology both solves and creates problems with equal passion and creativity. In many cases the rush towards progress leads to a regress in quality, content and character of life.

So, technology and progress are not synonyms. I only hope that in this mad quest to learn, to discover, to improve, we don't improve ourselves into oblivion.

Wisdom understands the discipline of pacing. Knowing when to brake and when to accelerate. To discover life's momentum and to ride the surge. This may prove difficult as our age continually creates new ways to absorb our time. I speak with tongue in cheek, but recent research has shown that the average person will spend six months of their life at traffic lights, one year looking through office clutter, two years calling people who either aren't in or their number is engaged, eight months opening junk mail, five years in queues, six months changing nappies, seven years shopping, ten years eating, four years in the bathroom, one year having sex and twenty-three years sleeping. I should hasten to add that after that one year of strenuous activity, twenty-three years of sleep would be something entirely understandable!

Many of us feel a little bit like Henry Kissinger who once quipped: 'There can't be a crisis next week, my schedule is already full.' Time has begun to get too big for its boots. It haunts and intimidates and then grows even larger as it feeds off our fear and frustration. Jerry Seinfeld noted that we now use time as a measurement for distance: 'How far is it to the beach?' 'About 20 minutes.' Yet this analogy does not work in reverse. 'How long does it take to read this book? 'About 300km!'

So how have we got ourselves in this mess? What are the causes of the time crunch?

1. Loss of Margin

I am indebted to Richard Swenson for the term and concept of 'margin'.[1] He puts forward the thesis that we, more than any other age, live marginless lives. If anything goes wrong we have no time to spare. The traffic jam makes us late. The extra child makes us broke. We continually move faster but we have more places to go. This, in turn, creates a tendency to hyperlive: skimming across the surface of life, pausing only momentarily to take a quick photo so that we can look in detail at what we have missed.

We have been sold the lie that the more things we fit into the day, the more life we are experiencing. In fact, the opposite may be true. We need to stop more, think more and do less, lest our lives become too gaudy, like some over-decorated house where the tenants spend 90% of their energy on keeping things tidy. Minimalism and simplicity are more the order of the day if we want to escape the clutches of life-lag, that common complaint similar to jetlag whereby we feel we are merely spectators, watching rather than participating in each passing moment. So used, are we, to this sensation that it is only when we finally get a break, go on holiday and begin to wind down, do we realise that we have not been living; only marking time.

2. City Life

Over the last 100 years the shift from rural to urban has been well documented. With the introduction of better communication - faxes, e-mail, Internet and the like, we may see this trend reversed. The British comedy, 'The Good Life' hinted at it. 'Field of Dreams' reemphasised it and yet for the moment it is a hope for some, a fantasy for others. The reality is that the majority of us are addicted to city life.

I, too, am part of this throng and I feel that my country friends over-emphasise the differences. 'You can't see the forest for the trees,' they declare. 'You are travelling so fast you don't have time to look at the speedometer.' Country folk have always realised that city dwellers do not tend to enjoy life as much. Even as far back as 1889, Banjo Paterson, probably Australia's most famous poet, wrote of the differing experience of both country and city living thus:

'And the bush hath friends to meet him, and their kindly
voices greet him,
In the murmur of the breezes and the river
on its bars.
And he sees the vision splendid of the
sunlit plains extended,

And a wond'rous glory of the everlasting stars.
I am sitting in my dingy office, where a stingy
Ray of sunlight struggles feebly down between
the houses tall.
And the foetid air and gritty of the dusty, dirty city
Through the open window floating, spreads its
foulness over all.
And in place of lowing cattle, I can hear
the fiendish rattle
Of the tramways and the buses making
hurry down the street,
And the language uninviting of the
gutter children fighting,
Carries fitfully and faintly through the ceaseless
tramp of feet.
And the hurrying people daunt me, and their pallid
faces haunt me,
As they shoulder one another in their rush
and nervous haste.
With their eager eyes and greedy, and their stunted
forms and weedy,
For townsfolk have no time to grow, they have no
time to waste.'[2]

3. Technology

The futurists of the last couple of decades used to say that technology would give us more time. The reality is that we have more channels but less to watch. We move faster, yet we have more places to go. We can clean quicker, but there is more to clean. Life has sped up. As one writer rightly commented: 'The overnight letter, which was the speed innovation of the 80s, is now only used if you are not in a hurry.'[3]

I often wonder how Jesus would have handled the demands of technology. Would he have carried a pager or a mobile? Would he have travelled to meetings by plane or fast train? And if so, how much of the substance of His words would have been lost if the time to reflect and connect with God was eroded? Maybe, the sounds of our alarms and beepers drown out the quieter yet more significant voices in our life.

THREE PRINCIPLES FOR TIMELESS LIVING

1. Time is Precious

Our time on earth is a gift. It is both valuable and fleeting. It should not be rushed through in order to get to retirement when we can stop and enjoy it. For then, for many, it is too late. No, as the Book of Psalms rightly points out: 'Today is the day the Lord has made, let us rejoice and be glad in it'.[4] The concepts of seizing the day and sucking the marrow out of life are one's that wisdom would encourage.

Tennyson again from the poem Ulysees, puts it:

'How dull it is to pause, to make an end, To rust unburnish'd, not to shine in use! As tho' to breathe were life!'

The truth is, that which we find ourselves in is not a dress rehearsal. I must not wait to enjoy, to think, to savour, to live. Now is my time and killing time is not so much murder as it is suicide. I am not here suggesting that this means we should do more things, for that is to fall into the folly of the rushed. No, I am talking about an attitude towards the passing of the moments. One that is filled with curiosity and gratefulness. One that appreciates and savours. One that weighs each moment and dances lightly within it.

2. Know Your Purpose

'Teach us to number our days aright, that we may gain a heart of wisdom.'[5]

Once we can appreciate and celebrate the nature of time, we quickly begin to realise that the best use of the passing moment is to discover our purpose. Lee Iacocca put it this way: 'If you want to make good use of your time, you've got to know what's most important, and then give it all you've got.' The general feeling of waste and frustration, that can easily pervade our existence, is usually a result of purposeless living.

I cannot believe that we were designed for, or can discover ourselves with, haphazard wandering. It was Zig Ziglar, who said: 'I believe man was designed for accomplishment, engineered for success and endowed with the seeds of greatness.' The purpose-driven life can differentiate between activity and accomplishment, between scheduling and significance, between waste and wander. This is entirely different to the drop-out solution to the time crunch. 'Slow down, you move too fast, you've got to make the moment last.' This 'feeling groovy' was nothing more than escapism. No, life must not be avoided. To do so is both selfish and self-defeating. Life must be lived for ourselves and for others. The purpose-driven rather than the pleasure-driven life achieves both these ends.

3. Give More Time To Contemplation

Deep contemplation remains the source of every great change in life. Einstein used to just sit and think for much of the time. Even the word 'contemplation' has a healing ring to it.

The trouble with our age is that we are surrounded by that of little weight. We have been trained to think in the shallows. The vigour and the real discipline of concentration or meditation has by and large been lost. Yet maybe this has always been the case.

Thoreau wrote over hundred years ago:

'The mind can be permanently profaned by the habit of attending to trivial things, so that all our thoughts should be tinged with triviality.'[6]

It seems some things never change.

The art and the discipline of thinking must be cultivated for, as we have already discussed, it is a primary attribute of wisdom. (See Chapter 7.)

Time will continually try to escape from us, therefore we must grab it and use it. It does not hang around until we are ready to take advantage of it. As the old maxim says:

'Time waits for no man, but for a woman of 29 it has been known to wait for a little while!'

ENDNOTES

1 Richard Swenson, *Margin*, Navpress, Colorado Springs, 1992.

2 Selected by Richard Hall, *Banjo Paterson, His Poetry and Prose*, Alan & Unwin, Sydney, 1993, p 46.

3 Robert Kriegel, *If it ain't broke - break it!*, Warner Books, New York, 1991.

4 Psalm 118:24.

5 Psalm 90:12.

6 Thoreau, *Life Without Principle*, Folcroft Library, 1970.

Chapter 15
MONEY

Whenever I think about the word, 'lifestyles', I invariably hear the dulcet tones of Robyn Leach as he extols the Lifestyles of the Rich and Famous. This popular TV series gave us all insight into life at the top of the cashflow pile, yet many of us were not that impressed: there was something missing. The Lear jets and limousines are all very well but lifestyle runs deeper and fuller than the latest luxury cruise or Brioni suit. Many of the gorgeous houses featured in the series did not reflect the quality of life to be had within. Houses don't make homes and money is a poor substitute for the relational and human moments that hold the keys to heartfelt happiness and fulfilment.

The news this morning had as its main story the bush fires that swept through the Dandenong Ranges near Melbourne. A couple who had, overnight, lost their new multi-level house and all their possessions were remarkably still smiling: 'We still have the important things,' the lady said. 'Our greatest loss is the photos.' In the final analysis, happy memories count far more than home or contents.

I am, of course, not saying that money somehow inhibits lifestyle by its very presence. Money is a force that can be used for good or evil. The problem lies when we believe its publicity, worship its power and trust in its security. Money talks but it doesn't always tell the truth. The mirage of materialism is just this; positive cash flow alone will not solve our problems and make us strong. The power of ownership cannot be given over to the note and coin. Money, its abundance or its lack, should never control us. Unfortunately, for many, conditioned by our superficial culture, such a statement seems idealistic. 'I need more money, then I will be in control!' is a contradictory cry. The essence of the controlled life is that self-government must come first.

Whenever we are looking for something else to give us the control we need, we are simply handing on our responsibility. That which we serve becomes our master. We must take control. If we do not, then the hunger for sexual fulfilment or the longing for financial independence will call the shots and make our decisions. Priorities are then set, destinations preassigned and we, we simply go along for the ride hoping that somehow everything will be alright.

The out-of-control life is one that is deeply miserable. We often think it might be just us. No one else is complaining. So we keep following on hoping that things will change.

In the words of Biddulph:

'Many are just pretending they are happy, hoping that pretending will somehow make it true.'[1]

The message that money can't buy happiness is surprisingly well known, and is becoming more and more accepted these days. I'm not sure, of course, if this acceptance is as deep as it is broad. I mean, most would feel they would be happier with more cash. Yet it no longer holds the central place in our dreaming. Yale University's social scientist, Robert Lane, claims that we are entering a new 'post-materialist' age. He points to an increased concern for the environment, participation at work and different kinds of freedom. John Vineburg of Lotto, NSW, concurs: 'A lot of people say they will stop working when they win Lotto, but when they actually think about it, they generally don't.'[2] Vineburg tells a story of one winner who reputedly bought the factory he worked in, but then told his boss to keep it quiet while he continued at his old job.

One would think that awareness of the truth that money is not a panacea would be more understood and accepted by those who are already well-off. Yet it seems that amongst both rich and poor there are those who have an unhealthy attachment or regard for the dollar and, equally so, those who view this subject with even-keeled good sense. The danger for many who have incredible wealth is that they lose themselves and become swamped by the power and allure of their burgeoning bank accounts. The materialistic treadmill just gets faster and more and more assets translates into more and more worry. Yet many would have it no other way for their identity and esteem are linked to the zeros on their statements. As Rene Rivken, one of Australia's richest men, put it: 'If I lost my wealth tomorrow I would feel suicidal. There is no question about that because I would lose most of what is me.'

What then is wisdom's response to the issue of money? How does the wise of heart interpret and live in our society where the power of money cannot be denied or escaped from? The following guidelines are ones I think wisdom would point us towards.

1. Maintain A Sense Of Priority

Such a point is axiomatic, yet wisdom doesn't so much make it as lives it. One can easily nod the head in agreement but then one must operate in such a way that earning more dollars does not seem to be the purpose of life. The extra hours may be worth an extra $5000 over the year, but at what expense? Family and spouse don't pay by the hour. They pay in far more mysterious and richer ways. 'I wish I had spent more time at the office,' are words one rarely hears from those at death's door. Our spiritual and relational worlds pay rich dividends. Altruism rewards, but not in easily described or measurable ways. Maybe herein lies our plight. We are so used to adding things up and measuring worth by price, that that which lies beyond such pragmatic parameters is subconsciously regarded as valueless. Maybe if we concocted a system where time spent with the 6-year-old or the spouse was able to be valued correctly. How much is the relational moments in marriage or time enjoyed with our children worth? I think the hourly rate would probably be sky high. To consider such questions is merely to see our lives as they really are. Deep down we know our priorities, it's keeping them to the forefront, which is the key. As naturalist, Louis Agassiz, stated:

'I cannot afford to waste my time making money.'

It is clear, however, that we all generally need a certain amount of money to survive. We need clothing, food and warmth. But beyond this, money provides diminishing returns. David Myers points out in his study of wealth and well-being that the words of Jesus, 'Man cannot live by bread alone,' acknowledge that we do need bread, but when we have it other needs - to belong, to feel esteemed and so forth - come to the fore. (As psychologist Maslow's famous 'hierarchy of needs' pyramid recognises.) The second helping never tastes as good as the first.[3] The second million in its correlation to happiness is almost meaningless. When needs are met such things as philanthropy and responsibility should take precedence. Unfortunately, as the pages of the 'Robb Report' or 'Millionaire' magazines attest, there are more and more worthless things to spend our money on. Solid-gold taps or diamond-studded cat collars are grotesque. Diamonds and gold are fine, but when supply exceeds demand, and when money exceeds purpose, then the worst sides of human nature are seen.

2. Don't Demonise The Dollar

Wisdom would not, however, swing to the opposite extreme. Money is an important part of our lives. It wields great power and influence and wise people throughout history have attracted it and used it for great good. I mean, who would we rather have this influence? The wise or the foolish? The good or the evil? The churches or the casinos? The self-absorbed or those who desire to serve? Wisdom does not get guilty about having money, or overly concerned when it does not. It is simply seen for what it is, a means of exchange and a tool which gives its owner more options. Wisdom is aware of the dollar's danger, but is equally aware of the perils and pain of poverty. It refuses both materialism on the one hand and asceticism on the other. Wisdom just is. Like a rock it is strong and stable and the poverty or prosperity of circumstance cannot change its essential character.

3. Organise Your Financial Affairs

This book is not designed to be a financial planner, yet the philosophy behind such volumes is both wise and essential. The practice of saving, budgeting, and giving are all reflections of the wise handling of finances. I personally am thankful for the huge amount of material available on the market in this area. Ignorance can no longer be used as an excuse for lack of a financial strategy.

I think the problem more often lies in the fear of facing the truth. Budgets are nasty things. They tell us, by their brazen honesty and unavoidable good sense, to quit spending and start saving. If you are anything like me, that is often a message we don't want to listen to and it is a lot easier not to hear it if we keep all financial analysis under wraps.

4. Know Where Joy Comes From

The miserable rich are not uncommon, whereas the smile of Mother Teresa was one of her most charming attributes. Many scholars and writers have noted how joy tends to be tied to faith, family and friends rather than net worth. Third-world theologian, Gustavo Gutierrez, notes: 'The believing core have never lost their capacity for having a good time and celebrating despite the hard conditions in which they live.'

Thus we are not surprised to find laughter on the streets of Lahore or, for that matter, melancholy in Monaco. 'Show me one couple unhappy merely on account of their circumstances,' wrote Samuel Taylor Coleridge, 'and I will show you ten who are wretched from other causes.' King Solomon, thousands of years ago, makes this point well: 'It is better to live in the desert than in a mansion with a contentious woman.'4

Now, before I am accused of sexism, let me point out that if a female version of Solomon, Solomena, had been writing this aphorism then we would be referring, of course, to a contentious man! The point is that relational harmony is far more important to enjoying life than the place of abode. The tent will always beat the condominium if the inhabitants of the former get on and the inhabitants of the latter are fighting. One day, even the soap operas might realise this. I mean, who of us would like to live on 'Melrose Place' or in the famous ranch on the television hit of the 80s 'Dallas'? Suddenly 'Coronation Street' or Jerry Seinfeld's small apartment don't look so bad! Atmosphere not assets, spirituality not second homes, peace not power is where the real action is.

I think the most important point to grasp is that financial security or integrity is not based on externals: income or investments, capitalism or communism. The answer and the problem lie within. We must deal with our own nature. Greed, envy and esteem can easily turn our money management into a minefield.

Jacques Ellul makes the point well that capitalism and communism founder not so much on the system but on the fallibility of humanity. The perfect system will always go awry when we are part of the picture.

'I am well aware of Marxism's promise that moral life will change with economic circumstances. This hope is built on the presupposition that there is no such thing as human nature but only a human condition and that if individuals behave badly it is only because of bad economic conditions.'[5]

So we find we cannot escape our responsibility. Wisdom seeks no alibis. It realises that life is about deeper and richer things than notes and coins.

ENDNOTES

1   Steve Biddulph, *Manhood*, Finch Publishing, Sydney, 1994, p 11.
2   As reported, *Australian Financial Review*, September 20th, 1997.
3   David Myers, *The Pursuit of Happiness*, Aquarium Press, London, 1993, p 37.
4   Proverbs 21:19.
5   Jacques Ellul, *Money and Power*, Inter-Varsity, Illinois, 1984, p 13.

EPILOGUE

WISDOM

A PERSONAL JOURNEY

*'We can be knowledgeable with other men's knowledge
but we cannot be wise with other men's wisdom.'*
Montaigne

Now, at the end of this volume, this truth that
Montaigne so clearly expresses, is our bane. If I want
to learn about Somerset Maugham or Sauternes I
only have to pick out a book and read. Knowledge is
not only available but, in our times, extremely accessible.

Yet the getting of wisdom does not follow this pattern. All a book on it can do is whet the appetite or
give the lay of the land. Wisdom itself is reserved for
the individual. It cannot be gained by perusing the
Internet or visiting the library. The intelligentsia can
miss it, while the street cleaner can discover it.
Enlarged cerebrum or classical education help little.
Only persistence, desire and depth of character lead
to it.

198

It is accessible for the desperate alone. Unlike the Holy Grail, it is not laying in wait at the end of the long trek, but like sore feet and happy memories, is given along the trail.

All we can do is continue on. The road is both bright and tough. Yet the hilled horizon up ahead, beckons.

> 'The road goes ever on and on,
> Down from the door where it began.
> Now far ahead the road has gone,
> And I must follow if I can,
> Pursuing it with eager feet,
> Until it joins some larger way
> Where many paths and errands meet.
> And whither then? I cannot say.'[1]

ENDNOTES

1   J.R.R. Tolkien, *The Fellowship of the Ring*, George Allen &
    Unwin Ltd., London, 1920, p 44.

ACKNOWLEDGEMENTS

The writing and production of a book is never solely the work of one person. I therefore want to thank Penny Webb for her constant encouragement and consistent work in transferring my barely legible script into pages of error-free print (we hope!).

Jonene Thompson and Lorna Bolwell who worked from the many micro-cassettes of my musings.

Mark Pomery who is contagiously optimistic and convincing in his attitude that lots of people will want to read all this.

My wife, Heather, for loving me and believing in me.

The waterfront apartments in Queenstown, New Zealand. And finally, to God who designed those mountains and lakes thus providing an excellent stress-free environment for writing a book.

ABOUT THE AUTHOR

Phil Baker is one of Australia's leading speakers, who has the ability to combine solid content with a practical, humorous and dynamic delivery.

He is also the author of several other books, including the best seller;

'SECRETS OF SUPER ACHIEVERS'.

Having been born in England, raised in New Zealand, he now resides in Perth, Western Australia where he pastors a contemporary church, Riverview Church, Burswood, which attracts over 2000 people every Sunday.

Phil is married to Heather and they have three girls, Jazmin, Temily and Isabel.

If you are interested in Philip Baker speaking for your group, or any of his other publications, please contact:

Webb & Partners
PO Box 1339
SOUTH PERTH 6951
WESTERN AUSTRALIA
Telephone/Facsimile (08) 9367 2190

Please send me:

✔ Philip Baker's **BEST SELLER,**
☐ **'SECRETS OF SUPER ACHIEVERS'** $16.95_{ea}

(Please insert quantity required in the box.)

✔ Additional copies of:
☐ **'WISDOM -**
The Forgotten Factor of Success' $16.95_{ea}

(Please insert quantity required in the box.)

✔ Plus Postage

Name _____

Address _____

_____

Postcode _____

Phone _____ Fax _____

Please Debit my Credit Card:
☐ Mastercard   ☐ Visa   ☐ Bankcard

Card Number:
☐☐☐☐ ☐☐☐☐ ☐☐☐☐ ☐☐☐☐

Expiry Date:

_____

Signature:

_____

Webb & Partners
PO Box 1339
SOUTH PERTH 6951
WESTERN AUSTRALIA
Telephone/Facsimile (08) 9367 2190